GW00384121

THE BACKSTABBER'S GUIDE

edited by ANNIE JONES

Illustrated by Bryn

Published by
OWL PRESS
P.O.Box 315, Downton, Salisbury, Wiltshire, SP5 3YE

Origination by Ex Libris Press, 1 The Shambles, Bradford on Avon, Wiltshire.
Printed and bound in Great Britain by A.Wheaton and Co. Ltd., Exeter.
Cover printed in Great Britain by Salisbury Printing Company Ltd., Salisbury, Wiltshire.

British Library Cataloguing in Publication Data:
The Backstabber's Guide
I. Jones, Annie II. Mitchell, Austin, *1934* -
828.91409

ISBN 0 9515917 2 X

ACKNOWLEDGEMENTS

This book could never have been produced without the help and advice of the following people: Ruth Arnold, Sam Austin, Mathew Dryden, Ian Foxley, Stephan Hopkinson, Brian Hilliard, Catherine Jones, Melanie Masson, Austin Mitchell, Roda Morrison, Annie Musgrove, Jason Nissé, Fran Parkinson, Sheila Parry, Richard Steward, Paula Webb, Richard West and Christian Wolmar. Many thanks to everyone involved and to those with whom they live for putting up with our incessant badgering and harranguing for help.

The Editor would like to add special thanks to Ruth who burnt many a midnight candle for her assistance in the preparation of the manuscript.

FOREWORD
by Julian Critchley M.P.

Could it be a back-handed compliment to have been asked to write a foreword to *The Backstabber's Guide*? And to do it for free? I could, of course, damn this small volume with the faintest of praise, by giving it the lazy schoolmaster's comment 'very satisfactory'. But that would be to stab the enterprise in the back. However, I shall do no such thing. This is a witty volume which tells of the progress of many pilgrims who wish to rise to the very top of their professions. It is written with Tory backbenchers, ambitious clergymen, and venal journalists in mind. Not even doctors escape the lash. In fact, it is a ladder let down into the pit out of which, had I read it twenty years ago, I might have climbed unerringly to the post of Assistant Postmaster General.

The authors of this handy guide reveal all the tricks that are necessary for achieving promotion, and they go some way to solving the mystery of why nice guys invariably come last. I hasten to add that the rule applies to all of us, save for John Major. I had more than enough trouble with his predecessor.

What comes out of reading this compendium is the faintly depressing conclusion that success does depend in having the right background. Failing that you need to use every devious method at your disposal to reach your goal. If this involves toadying to one's superiors, telling tales out of school, and even working hard occasionally, it is a small price to pay for promotion. I do hope the publishers will send copies to all newly-elected M.P.s, provincial journalists who want to work on a national newspaper, and to the newly-ordained: they stand in need of all the help they can get. The uncharitable might Christen this book, "the shits' guide to success", but I shall have none of it. I have not sat on the Tory backbenches for a quarter of a century without realising the truth of its contents. Bag-carriers of the world unite; you have nothing to lose but the love of your neighbour.

Julian Critchley

Et tu, Brute.

Shakespeare

CONTENTS

THE BACKSTABBER'S GUIDE TO:

MOTHERHOOD

by Annie Jones

ENTER BACKSTABBER

Backstabbing begins in the cradle and continues to the grave. Inevitably, we will all encounter at least one or more examples of Backstabber during the course of our own lives (but whether we recognise them in time is another matter). No-one can be totally blind to the ploys of these pushy and ambitious men and women - hell-bent on their own promotion, vain beyond belief, whose idea of window-shopping is looking at their reflection to check their appearance (and to make sure that no-one is standing behind them). Totally lacking in Christian virtues, they are the ones who only let you lead the way if they know there is an open manhole ahead. Many Backstabbers are created by nature, but many more have been groomed by their mothers from birth.

These mothers are Backstabbers *manqués* themselves, and they long for the day when they can bask in their offspring's success - a scholarship here, a first class degree there, and ultimately *at least* one award in the Honours Lists. Boasting of their children's achievements is their favourite dinner-party topic. On hearing that Camilla has done so well that she's been accepted at an Anglian Redbrick, they retort with glee that Charles goes up, as expected, to Oxbridge in the Autumn. They simper 'I don't know who he inherits his brain from - it can't be me.' Oh no? Isn't that precisely why they gave up their own career? To ensure *exactly* this outcome! If a backstabbing mother doesn't automatically produce a future Backstabber, then she relentlessly sets about making one.

BEFORE YOU START

Backstabbing amongst mothers is a swiftly-learned art. It is learnt before any baby is born. Antenatal classes and coffee mornings are the nursery schools for mothers. It is here that mothers and mothers-to-be show off their ability to put on the right amount of weight, give up smoking and lie about how many glasses of wine they drink each week. It is the start of the career of one-upmumship. It takes no time at all for them to establish which group of mothers they will belong to. It is hardly surprising that expectant mothers who come with their partner in tow to learn the essentials of bathing the baby and changing nappies, are the earth mothers of the future who will bore dinner-party guests rigid with a blow-by-blow account of their child's progress at potty-training.

Motherhood comes as a not always altogether welcome surprise to some mothers. After four months of dieting and high-impact aerobics to get rid of their tummy, the penny finally drops. When their pregnancy test proves positive, they need to sit down with their last stiff G&T and cigarette to calm their nerves. As they are halfway through their pregnancy by now, motherhood and child development come as a source of continual surprise. These are the laid-back mothers of the future - they are always at least six months behind. While other mothers are frantically pushing their children to reach adolescence by the age of six, their children still have their dummies pinned onto their coats at school.

For other mothers, pregnancy is as well planned as a major battle campaign when no more blanks will be fired. There is a whole sector of the economy devoted to this end. Sophisticated and expensive tests are available to test not only if you are pregnant, but also when you should be bonking like a rabbit fitted with Duracell batteries to achieve maximum success. Your stamina is really put to the test when it comes to having a second child. When you already have a young family, an 'early night' is not so much a come-on as a necessity. Most couples go to bed to sleep rather than anything else. They reserve their sex life for birthdays and Christmas.

WRITING YOUR BIRTH PLAN

Many mothers like the birth to be as well planned as the conception. There is a library of books advising on birth plans and pain relief. Most perfect mothers-to-be insist on natural childbirth. This could mean giving birth in a bath, the sea or a Jacuzzi, but for most mothers it's just not practical to get their partner to strip off and get soaking wet in his lunch-break from the City. So as a good alternative, many mothers go in for a birth plan. Women's magazines devote pages to advising mothers on every aspect of birth - from who should be present to what sort of pain relief they want. For some first-time mothers, the idea that 'If it's painful it must be doing some good' is very appealing (they must be aerobics teachers). As a result, they often sign their birth plan to say they want no pain relief. Imagine the situation when - sixteen hours of torture later - they are screaming for pain relief and their partner intervenes waving a piece of A4 paper and saying 'Excuse me, but she says here that she wants NO pain relief.' (You can bet he won't be writing a plan when it comes to his vasectomy.)

BACKSTABBING ON THE WARD

After the birth there is plenty of opportunity to backstab on the ward. Some will recount with relish every ache and pain of their 48-hour labour, only to be swiftly cut down when you tell them yours only took half-an-hour and was as easy as shelling peas. One midwife put me in my place with a tale of how one mother was so fast the baby was practically born wearing her tights - 'It looked like a little bank-robber when it arrived.' She conjured up pictures of everyone having a jolly time in the labour room, laughing their socks off. How could you mention that it hurt just a teeny-weeny bit after that?

Next in order of swiping comes the weight of the baby. Every visitor you receive will want to know the weight, sex and name of the baby - in that order. The weight of your baby is exceedingly important. On the basis that big is best, your success as a mother depends on how heavy your baby is. Not only that, but giving birth to The Incredible Bulk is a cause of much admiration, as one wonders how it was gynaecologically possible. Presumably sex after that is like waving a torch in a blackout in the Albert Hall.

AS THE CHILDREN GROW UP

Backstabbing is usually at its fiercest amongst mothers of small children, as it is then that they tend to be thrown into each other's company at toddler groups, dancing classes and at the school gate. Backstabbing among mothers all rather depends on your perspective. In the task of bringing up one's children, everyone is an expert, and of course their way of doing things is the right way. The opportunities for criticising, bitching and getting the knife in are infinite - and a good thrust always makes you feel better.

The most ferocious Backstabbers are full-time mothers whose children are their life's work. They can't understand why anyone should want to have children if they're not going to look after them. Presumably this option doesn't extend to fathers.

MOTHERSPEAK

Mothers must quickly learn the basics of motherspeak if they are to survive in the cut and thrust of coffee mornings and baby-sitting circles. Here are a few terms to get started with:

Father - useful, though no longer essential, at conception;

Postnatal checkup - when your GP makes a damage assessment of your body;

Natural creativity - making a mess with paints all over the kitchen table;

Playgroup - where you send your toddler to cut, stick, paint and make a mess so you don't have to put up with it any longer at home;

Montessori schools - where you pay through the nose for children to make a mess;

Educational toys - expensive toys which offer your child some rewarding educational experience: full of numbers, colours, shapes and other worthy things and above all providing ten minutes' peace and quiet;

Tactile development - touching, squeezing and destroying

everything - this often includes both the child and you wearing his dinner;
Latching on - when babies try to breast-feed themselves from anyone and anything, including your mother-in-law's nose;
Child Allowance - payment by the Government for having children, which can be saved up to pay for necessities like the dog's quarantine or a week for yourself on a health farm.

DIFFERENT SORTS OF MOTHERS

While mothers come in all shapes and sizes, their attitude to child-care can be broadly divided into three main types. There are full-time mothers who put their children's interests first: their biggest dread is being stuck inside with the children all week. There are laid-back mothers who are totally relaxed: above all else they dread their children having to be anywhere on time. Finally there are career-break mothers who fit motherhood into weekends: they dread their children being ill, but even worse the nanny being ill.

FULL-TIME MOTHERS

Every minute of their day is spent creating a stimulating and worthwhile experience for their children. Even the sandwiches for tea are made by the children and cut into the shape of smiling faces. Their whole day is one mad rush from nursery school, to feeding the ducks, to playing in the park, to having tea with their friends, to going to violin lessons. They spend all weekend going swimming and on trips to the zoo. Their problem is not what to choose to do in a day but how to fit it all in. They can't have more than two children otherwise it's too much of a scramble in the car to take the children to Tumble Tots, ballet and tea at McDonald's. They positively relish cramming as much into their days as possible. Half the country's economy depends on them spending money on toys, clothes, outings and food for their children. There are books, videos and even classes on how to be the perfect parent. After such a rewarding start to life, school must be a real let-down for their children.

Their language is punctuated by 'Oh, darling, don't do that' as the children jump around madly on your sofa in their Wellington boots. Theirs are positive comments like 'Oh, darling, isn't it wonderful, it must be a rainbow' as they look at a soggy, splodgy mess from play-school.

Full-time mothers are not averse to a bit of backstabbing - far from it; they positively revel in it. It usually takes the form of who can cram the most into their week for their children, and who can find the most novel rewarding experiences for them - like violin lessons for the under-threes or aromatherapy sessions for two-year-olds. When you try and enroll your own children you invariably find that waiting lists are completely full until well into the next century, by which time you'll be a grandmother. When you casually let it slip that your child is learning to write his name, you learn that their's could practically write an entire novel while still in his cot. At every stage of development they have made sure that their child is well advanced for his age. So when the Health Visitor comes round to do a developmental check, all that practice of building towers with bricks pays off - their child passes with flying colours. They're already booking him in for his MENSA test. Of course when the child goes to school you can guarantee that he will be either gifted or dyslexic . . . never average.

It is the full-time mother who is washing the home-made play-dough off the floor at 10 o'clock at night after the children have finally gone to bed. Their bedtime tends to be later than most because they are kept up for 'quality time' with Daddy. This usually involves him in changing a nappy or reading what Spot is up to in the chicken shed for the twentieth time. Although he'd rather be slumped in a chair with a beer and the FT, he dare not show it.

Full-time mothers made sure they were well prepared for their role and probably did lots of yoga during pregnancy. They will certainly have insisted in their birth plan that they did not want any form of pain relief. They might be one of nature's full-time mothers, but they insist that their partners become 'natural' parents too. They will have gone to antenatal classes and learned breathing exercises . . . very useful later on when changing a nappy. Most full-time mothers breast-feed their babies - many until at least a year old. These mothers regard giving up breast-feeding as a failure second only in importance to having pain relief during labour.

LAID-BACKMOTHERS

Not all mothers are as conscientious in their life's work of bringing up children as full-time mothers. There exists a school of thought which believes that left alone, apart from occasionally being fed, children will bring themselves up. This attitude has a lot to merit it. You can lie around all day reading esoteric novels, while the children rampage about eating anything from last night's left-overs to the cat's breakfast. The children invariably survive and you can expand your mind.

THE FAMILY WASH

The laid-back mother is an easy target for other groups of mothers. They fail to understand how she gets away with doing so little for her children. While they are rushing madly from ballet classes to Brownies, she is busy making chutney in the kitchen while her children sit watching television. Her children's idea of an out-of-school activity is having a quick fag on the way home. But if you have ever accompanied a laid-back mother on an outing to the supermarket or shopping in town, you will know why it's safer for her to stay at home. It's the children's responsibility to stay with their mother, not the other way round. If they don't stay close to her in shops, she will wander off to look at something and they will have to find their way to the lost children's department yet again. By the time they are eight they will have been through it countless times: knowing their name and address is a priority. After all, they've been yo-yo-ing up and down in lifts on their own for years.

The trick with laid-back mothers is not to let them visit you. Always go to them. This may sound a bit hard, but after they've called on you a few times, you'll know why. Picture the likely situation. You invite a mother and her five- and two-year-old round for tea to play with your two children. You expect to have a relaxing afternoon, chatting about nothing in particular while the children play. How wrong could you be? Instead of having two children to watch, you've now got four, as they all slop their Ribena over your carpet and stuff half-eaten biscuits under the sofa. Her children will take everything out of every drawer in every bedroom and then go and play in the airing cupboard. In seconds, they will turn shelves of pressed linen Benetton would be proud of into a heap of jumble. At first you fret over the spilt drinks, but then you give up on the mess and become laid-back for the afternoon too. With a great deal of self-control you manage to overcome the itching feeling in the palm of your hand when the children raid your make-up and daub lipstick all over the duvet. Then you firmly grit your teeth when the children smear their snotty noses on the television screen, and you watch the mother change a stinking nappy on your kitchen table.

You will have noticed with irritation that the children of many laid-back mothers do not display the usual range of tantrums.

Her children don't throw wobblies on the floor at the supermarket check-out when, yet again, they find that the sweets are not there for them. They probably have never had to stamp their feet or throw themselves rigid in their push-chairs for anything. Laid-back mothers don't give in to children's demands because they simply don't notice that they are making any. Rules don't really exist. If they want chocolate spread sandwiches to eat in bed at 9 o'clock they just get up and make them. It seems like a kind of heaven to other children brought up under a more authoritarian regime.

Fathers need to be laid back too if they are to avoid living in a continual state of shock about what the children have done. A classic case was reported recently in a national newspaper: the father of one three-year-old must have been more than a little furious when he discovered the fire brigade had been called to rescue his eight Dobermann puppies from the drainage system beneath his house. The mother was reported as saying that she thought she had heard a lot of flushing in the bathroom.

Rather than wade unannounced and unnoticed through piles of plastic toys in the hallway, most fathers ring up from work to say 'I'll be leaving in twenty minutes'. This gives even the most laid-back mothers time to begin the Herculean task of sorting out the children, putting on the supper and clearing a path to the front door.

CAREER-BREAKMOTHERS

While most mothers, in rare moment of honesty, might wish they were doing something else with their lives other than looking after the children (you know - the 'If only I hadn't had the children I could have been an astronaut' syndrome), there are some mothers who manage to combine their career and children. Many reach a kind of mid-life crisis - 'If I don't have a baby now I never will'. The trouble is that once you have proved that the plumbing works, had one and seen what it looks like, there it is for life. You can't have them on a sale or return basis, otherwise the hospitals would be overflowing with two-year-olds throwing tantrums.

The first shock for most career-break mothers is that having survived all week on very little sleep, you don't get weekends off. Many a high-powered executive mother is worn down to a snivelling wreck by a few weeks of sleepless nights. The transformation is swift, and you are quickly recognisable by your zombie-like state. Most days, your main aim is to get dressed by lunchtime, drink copious cups of coffee and watch a whole episode of *Neighbours*. Any spare time you have is spent reading baby books and wondering if life will ever be the same again.

Then you remember that, after all, maternity leave isn't for ever, and soon you will be able to get back to the challenge of your career. You are fairly immune to the backstabbing of other mothers, and you vaguely wonder what these other mothers do all day and why they all seem to know each other. Maternity leave is an important time for interviewing nannies, calculating their National Insurance contributions and wondering if they will end up earning more than you. It is a time for doing Jane Fonda-type exercises and working out how to fit all that flab into your executive suits.

Career-break mothers become adept at separating work from home. Once they have got rid of the odd give-away - like sick on the shoulder of their jumper and baby food in their hair - they can get on with their busy day. The hardest part is getting out of the house in the morning. They have usually done a full day's work before they get to the office: they will have fed three children breakfast simultaneously, prepared lunch, tea and supper, tested the eldest child's spelling and ironed the youngest child's party dress. As for backstabbing other mothers, they haven't got time for that. They are too busy surviving their own hectic schedule. They invariably decide that what they need is a wife.

The main problem career-break mothers face is guilt. They feel guilty when they are away from the children, and guilty when they are with them and wish they weren't. Just at the time of day when other mothers want to ignore their children, career-break mothers come in, take over from the nanny and, with a stiff drink in one hand, listen with rapt attention to their two-year-old's garbled tale of how, yet again, she managed to lock nanny out of the front door. By the time you have worked out what she is trying to tell you, the nanny will have legged it off home or up to her room. Still, at least she didn't prang the car or walk out. That will probably happen tomorrow.

DESCRIBING YOUR CHILD

Whatever type of mother you are, it is essential that you learn to make the most of your children's qualities and achievements. Children must never be run down in public, and the expressions which follow can help you give as much credit as possible to your child, even when at first you can think of few positive things to say. (This list will also be useful later on for interpreting school reports.)

On Personality:

Creative - scribbles on walls and furniture
Inventive - lies
Expressive - yells all day in his cot
Affectionate - clingy
Persistent - whinges and whines
Tactile - fiddles with willies (not necessarily his/her own)
Placid - thick as a brick
Slow - a complete cabbage

On Looks:

Slender - skinny
Solid - fat
Unusual - I've never seen anything quite like it before

On Behaviour:

Independent - makes a bolt for the door every time it is opened
Determined - stroppy
Confident - shows off
Knows her own mind - a right little madam
Difficult - a real little sod
Strong - destroys everything in sight
Doesn't know his own strength - beats the shit out of other children (Prambo)

THE HALLMARKS OF OTHER CHILDREN

One thing is for sure: mothers can judge exactly which socio-economic group a family comes from just by the child's clothes. The less money you have, the more fashionable their clothes. And as for old money, their children are always kitted out in hand-me-downs - after all, they only need play-clothes fit for rampaging around the estate: everything else is second-hand anyway - the house, the furniture, the pram and the christening robe. We would call them antiques, but to say so would be to stab oneself in the foot: they would just say it was something grandma had turned out of the attic.

For many mothers, children are the fashion accessory of the late Twentieth Century. How else could designer clothes manufacturers survive if we did not spend millions on designer babywear which is guaranteed to be covered in sick, food and grime within ten minutes and outgrown in ten days? Most designer babies hardly make it out of their designer prams for more than ten minutes a day anyway, as their mothers spend so much time wheeling them about as they scour the boutiques for the latest fashions.

Above all, children's parties are the great melting pot for the different types of mothers. Once children have reached school age they will invite whom they like to their birthday parties, disregarding the protests of their mothers. Consequently, darling little Camilla in her velvet headband and Sarah-Louise in her party frock will be leaping up and down during musical bumps next to Tracey in her shocking pink and orange two-piece with lime-green cowboy fringe. You can also be sure that the only present little Camilla will really fall upon at the party is not the aesthetically pleasing solitaire set made from 27 different species of non-endangered wood, but that nauseating little horse complete with its own glue factory. But whatever your feelings, you must be sure to grit your teeth and enthuse over the presents and outfits because you can be utterly certain that if you let your views be known, the children will all mention the subject loudly just as Tracey's mother comes to collect her: 'My mummy says that the pink pony is awful, and please, Mrs Adams, what's an abattoir? Will the pony like it there?' If you attempt a denial, you will only make things worse.

It is at this stage that most mothers decide a birthday treat is infinitely preferable to a party, so henceforth you arrange an outing to the pantomime, the ballet or a theme park, when you can legitimately restrict numbers with 'We only have room in the car for Letitia and Harry, darling, so I'm afraid Sharon can't come this year. We'll invite her next year.' (Like hell we will.)

With the demise of the birthday party in favour of the birthday treat, your contact with other mothers will become almost non-existent. Once your offspring have reached the ripe old age of 6 or 7, you cease to care whether yours are the only children in their class who can (or can't) tie their own shoe laces or do joined-up writing. In fact with any luck you will have got yourself back into a decent job and will be far too knackered, after a day's hard graft, to waste your breath gassing in the playground. You will have to save your energies for the full day's worth of housework that awaits you at home.

THE UNKINDEST CUT OF ALL

Now that you are removed from the company of other mothers and children, the only hazard you have to face are the grandparents. It's odds on that the only time little Katie wants to know where babies come from, or William wants to mention the sex drive of the cat, will be when the wrinklies are about. Last weekend, Grandpa was blasted out of his afternoon rest by Katie holding up her teddy and announcing 'Teddy's a girl.' 'How do you know?' 'Because she hasn't got a willy.' Too late for you to mutter darkly about the National Curriculum and its modern approach to science: in your parents' eyes you have completely failed to 'bring up the children properly'. You blush. Stabbed by your own child.

BACKSTABBING *AD INFINITUM*

Once you have recognised that backstabbing amongst mothers is endemic, you will realise the answers to some of life's *real* puzzles. Such as, the reason full-time mothers stick 'Baby on Board' signs in their cars is to warn other drivers that they cannot be held responsible for their driving when deafened by 100 decibels of screaming; that stair-gates are to get career-break mothers fit for the day when the escalators fail on London underground; and that safety catches on cupboards are to stop laid-back mothers resorting to the gin bottle. The mystery of why the bough broke in 'Rock a bye baby on the tree-top' is solved: that was no act of nature - sibling rivalry had a hand (with a saw) in it. It will then come as no surprise to learn that backstabbing mothers produce the real backstabbers of the professions. Where else could the artful, sly and overly-ambitious within our society come from?

It is undeniably true that some are born to it, but other Backstabbers are (wo)man-made. They learn their trade first at their mother's breast, and then at her knee - praised incessantly for their every effort - first smiles, first words, first steps and first successes on the pot are all showered with lavish praise. Accustomed to their mothers blowing their trumpet as well as their nose, with a formidable pedigree and a superabundance of aggression, they are totally self-motivated and are destined from birth to become the next generation of Backstabbers:

> 'Mirror, mirror on the wall,
> Who's the brightest star of all?'
> 'Not you, you rotten little rat,
> You don't know what you're playing at.
>
> 'If you want power and you want money,
> A life replete with milk and honey,
> If these all be your aims in life,
> Forget the rules and wield the knife!'

POLITICS

by Austin Mitchell, MP

WHY POLITICS?

Aspiring Backstabbers should consider Politics as the best field for perfecting the art. It can be boring, with low rewards compared to the Bar or the boardroom. It certainly does not fulfil the dreams of *News of the World* readers, or the inhabitants of Norman Lamont's basement. Its sex life is decidedly DIY - with little of the D. Yet consider it as a leisure occupation, or part-time relief from the compulsory goodness of being a social worker, Archbishop of Canterbury, or some other lowly job where good behaviour is enforced.

In Politics, your interpersonal assassination skills can be developed, your character hardened (as there is no longer cause to fight over policies), and your art form practised - all in a field where you only need six 'O' levels and an IQ of 90+ to rocket to the top. Intelligence, skill and finesse are rare commodities in Politics. Possess any of them, and you will succeed even more quickly - although you should also consider whether you could not do better in the real world. The same goes for taste, sensitivity, discretion and sympathy for fellow human beings; you will need none of them in Politics.

The public esteem of politicians is as low as that of bank robbers, door-to-door condom salesmen or Saddam Hussein. So choosing Politics might seem about as attractive as contracting AIDS in order to meet Princess Di. Think seriously about your objectives and yourself. Yourself first - the only position for politicians. Are you a devious scrounger, intent on getting as much as possible for as little effort as possible? If you have half a mind to go in for Politics, do so. Half a mind is all you'll need! There is no guaranteed access to big money in Politics, but look at Nigel Lawson: unable to produce an economic miracle for the country , he had no difficulty in conjuring one for himself. It is also the only career with no retirement age. Senility is no disqualification - indeed it may even be an advantage. Manny Shinwell drew a politician's salary until he was 100; the Lords and Commons have some of the best paid geriatrics in the world, all kept in carefully heated surroundings to prolong inactive life, often until well after brain death. Do you understand nothing but think you know it all? Then it's Politics for you.

PLUSES AND MINUSES

There are drawbacks. It can be hard work if you make the mistake of believing in what you are doing. In the Labour Party, Marx is dead, Crosland is dead, and Tony Benn isn't feeling too good. In the Tory Party, Mrs Thatcher's demise has restricted ideology to the 'Will Ye No Come Back' group - a kind of political padded cell. Now politicians can safely dispense with both principles and ideology.

Politics is a platform on which you can say - or do - more or less what you want. The only requirement is to have no *public* connection with sex, Pamella Bordes, or any chemical or physical joys unknown to the police. Public appearance is all. In *private* anything goes. You are authorised - indeed required - to appear on MPTV from the Chamber saying anything you want, however libellous. You are a media star. Character assassination for a fee is open to you as a vocation. Whatever you say, someone has to listen. Wherever you go, you go first class; wherever you park, you claim privilege. And if you want the most travel - and the best meals as well - become a Member of the European Parliament.

POWER IN BRITAIN'S DEMOCRACY

No-one really possesses power in Britain's messy, divided, declining democracy (except Rupert Murdoch, who only has it because he does not live here). Yet if anyone comes anywhere near to power it's you: the politician. Political power is a lottery, and only politicians have tickets. You are bound to hold a fragment of it at some stage, however incomplete it is and however incompetent you are. It is all a matter of luck in such an egalitarian art that everyone gets a little bit - even the Liberals. Politics is a continuous process of shake-up, designed to spread everything - power, place, and particularly blame. Elections are a gamble, but eventually all parties will enjoy their share of power (though some may have to wait until the next millennium). A governing party has to have over 300 MP's. Over 100 of those will have only just been elected, and another 100 will be too drunk, stupid or senile to do anything useful except vote as directed. Thus your prospects are more than good - they are inevitable.

THE SECRET OF POLITICS

The first rule of Politics, Chance the gardener once told me, is 'Being There'. Draw your salary, and wait. The perfect job. Particularly for those with little prospect of any other. So if you feel overtaken by those who are brighter, better and smarter than you (i.e. most people) then you can use Politics to turn the tables on them, boss them around, rule over them, and - if necessary - bankrupt and unemploy them, or conscript them for war as well. The second rule is 'Grab' - power, ideas, jobs or anything else. Politics has neither precedence nor patents. The third rule is 'Conform' - you will be disqualified if you are brilliant, unusual or different.

It is preferable to start young - the younger the better. Eighteen is a good age. Any older and you might be expected to achieve something before you go into Politics, so giving time for your failings to emerge. In the bad old days, it was expected that people would rise to a senior position in their town, union, or professional tree, before they went into Parliament. Not any more. Nowadays politicians are professionals, not gentlemen (a species as useful in Parliament as Cyril Smith at hang-gliding). So do *anything* to fill in time before you get elected, even badly paid and boring jobs - or just draw the dole and aim for the sympathy vote. All are useful preparations for Politics. Sit there. Wait there. Ready for something to happen. TO YOU. Don't try to make it happen (that way lies Edwina Currie and failure). It will.

CHOOSING YOUR OWN LABEL

Once you have decided that you are base, greedy, bumptious and thoroughly unpleasant (and therefore a natural politician), you must pick a brand label. Do not join a minor party. All you will get is the pleasure of making a fool of yourself for four weeks and then being charged £1,000 in a lost deposit. Standing for Parliament on a ticket which cannot win is clearly crazy - like endless kerb-crawling and no sex.

In Scotland, the SNP is the obvious choice, and it has the virtue that you don't have to decide whether you are really Labour or Tory. But you must have good knees (for putting in groins, not kilts). No use joining the SDP - not even if you are David Owen. It is played by the Sealed Knot Society these days. As for the Liberal Democrats, they are for people who cannot decide what they - or their sexual preferences - really are.

To get anywhere you must be Labour or Tory. But avoid extremism in either - particularly in the Labour Party, where socialism is now an expellable offence. If you hope for more power for longer, then join the Tories. To get into power, the Labour Party have to dress up as the only party which can win in Britain: a conservative party. Having run out of things to do, Labour is now dedicated only to stopping the Tories undoing what Labour had done already; while the Tories themselves have given up the desire to do anything else. Thus the constitution is back to normal, with both parties led by a Tory, both opposed to socialism, neither anxious to do anything except help their friends covertly. It does not matter which party you choose. Your real choice is just how conservative do you want to be? Politics is a transvestite orgy, and no-one is sure any longer just who is wearing what, and what belongs to whom - the ideal climate for Backstabbers, as parties argue more and more about less and less, and the knives can flash anywhere.

YOUR BACKGROUND

To choose your party, answer these basic questions: How much money do you have? How much do you want? Answer 'Lots' to both questions and you are Conservative - the party of those who have made it, and those on the make. Tories are all members of the same tribe, all coming (or pretending to come) from similar backgrounds and schools. If you pretend, like Jeffrey Archer, they will accept you because now most are too jumped-up to know the difference. You can even come from humble origins - provided you proclaim it often, like Norman Tebbit. There is little *noblesse* and no *oblige* in the Tory Party today. Ordinary people are welcomed in the same way that museums accept exhibits and have one great advantage: nobodies are harder-working than somebodies. The last three Tory leaders have all come from humble origins - grammar schools, grocers and the Lambeth Labour Exchange.

Labour is for people with hearts bigger than their pockets or brains. A small handful of the Labour Party are wealthy and feel guilty about it. The rest are genuinely naïve or worthy: teachers, or journalists or members of the Struggling Masses and Related Trades Unions, all working for the Polytariat. It helps to be in a trade union: it will buy you a seat (for Labour still has 'rotten boroughs'), pay your travelling expenses, donate money to local parties to select you, and pay costs to them afterwards.

THE BACKSTABBER'S GUIDE TO SELECTION

First understand the psychology of party members. To be in a political party is a badge of abnormality . . . like leprosy. No normal person is going to attend the boring meetings and take part in the puerile activities upon which parties depend. You are in the party either to rule the world or to sit on top of it for a while, however short: so you are odd, like your fellow Members - but it's no use telling them that. Observe the formalities: never laugh; tell no jokes; take everyone at face value. However tasteless, stupid, prejudiced or vicious they may be, you need them. You also need perseverance, and the kind of brass nerve which can interpret every set-back as a commendation and every obstacle as an aid. What is being tested is your ability to conform and your tolerance of stupid time-wasting. Eventually you will get selected, but adherence to some basic rules will accelerate the process:

NIMBY - 'Not In My Back Yard' covers anything from dog dirt and nuclear waste to getting selected for a political party. People used to select local men whom they could assess first - usually men of dignity, achievement and experience who had made some contribution to the area. Today, the odds are stacked against a local candidate: he is known - so are his faults and failings. He is unlikely to impress those who remember the missing threepence from the Sunday school trip. In communities everything is remembered. As an outsider, your faults and failings won't be known. The forged letters of commendation and false news clippings you bring in your support will never be checked.

NEVER BE A FRONT RUNNER - The name of the game is to be the dark horse, who can come in and nobble the leaders. Aim to be the Great Healer, rather than the Great Heel.

NO IMPOSITIONS - Never look as if you have been imposed - even if the party leader is your brother-in-law, the national officials of the party have accepted bribes running into thousands to promote your candidacy, and local officials have fiddled a short-list of one. Present yourself as an underdog - a man of the people - and look vulnerable. Local parties resent being told to do anything (even to follow party policy).

GIMMICKS - Have several. Show none! If you are a woman, it is difficult to get selected; but if you *are* and *do*, insist that you have no intention of burning your bra. That might disappoint the men, but reassures the party women (who would collapse if the fashion caught on). If you are 18 and totally immature, do not say that geriatrics dominate the party. Locally, it is almost certainly true, but they are not going to like you for it, so emphasise that you have a lot to learn and that they can teach you (they will interpret this as an invitation to corrupt). Never imply that you are God's gift - or even his Son. It did not help David Icke. However stupid the selectors may be they know a nut when they see one.

NO BACKSTABBING - Selections are initiation rites for the life of hypocrisy to come, so backstab like fury - but never be seen to do so. At this early stage, get your friends to dig up any dirt they can find on your opponents, then you can denounce the resulting nasty rumours about their personal habits and sexual proclivities. You, of course, are above that kind of malevolent slander (at least publicly).

AIM FOR STATESMANSHIP - In the Labour Party, dress *à la 'Follette'* in a Marks & Spencer or Burton's suit - both slightly superior to that of the average party member but, like theirs, having big bottoms. For a Tory member, something better is essential - but nothing ostentatious or Armani. Power-dressing is for women. Shoulders wide enough to stop them coming through the door will command attention and remind everyone they are as good as any man. Yet a woman has to convey the impression of an intermediate sex: no threat to husbands *or* wives! Unlike the male candidates, the selectors are not thinking of marrying you off to their offspring.

BE HUMBLE - Airs and graces impress neither party. A genuinely upper-class accent is now alien to both , and will be recognised and resented before the plums have fallen from your mouth - particularly among the Tories, who have become thoroughly Tebbitised: their best accent is now North London. Any hint of pedagogy is usually the kiss of death. But Labour sometimes selects teachers (this being the only profession for which Parliament represents a step up the income ladder), although they are loathed on both sides of the House for the memories they resurrect: so if you are one, speak roughly - but without swearing (that gives the game away).

THE SELECTION SPEECH

Work on this until perfect. Practise it and memorise it. A selection speech is forever . . . although it should not seem like that at the time. It must be carefully crafted to blend the following ingredients:

LOCAL TOUCHES - Pathetic gratitude at being considered by the constituency; your connections with the place (preferably invented); how it has changed for the better (if your own party is in power locally) or for the worst (if it is not); how you are looking forward to making your home here - although in these days of equality you will have to consult your 'partner' (a word not to be used in the Tory Party).

PERSONAL HISTORY - Not so much your own - though in the Labour Party you should hint at zeal for social services and helping people, and in the Tories allude to your ability at making money or climbing a professional ladder. Do not give precise details. Just indicate your devotion to the political cause and deep conviction of its rightness.

POLICY - Your party is divided into a hundred factions. To espouse one is to alienate all the others. Yet you need to be on a band-wagon that is going to win. So attack the other party. Parties exist to hate the other side, and if hatred didn't exist they would have little to say. Policies are like platforms: useful for getting on the train but not to be taken with you.

PEDDLE THE ORTHODOXIES - In the Tory Party, demand the death penalty for crimes against property, criminal sanctions on the trade unions, and discipline in other people's homes. Attack the BBC and the popular press - always exempting the *Daily Mail* and the *Daily Express*. In the Labour Party, attack the Common

Market, the Common Agricultural Policy, Rupert Murdoch, *The Sun* and the 'media' (pronounced with a 'j'). In both parties, a bit about the environment will send them to sleep but do no harm.

THE VISION - The point where you project what the hatchet-faced collection of drabs in front of you want into a glowing future. A successful vision proffers inducements to party members: legalised bribery is still unthinkable (like drive-in brothels provided on the NHS), so bribes are disguised as tax cuts for the Tories, and vast benefit and spending increases for Labour. Your vision is that it will be *your* special mission in life to benefit *them*.

END OF SPEECH - You now have to answer questions. So prepare yourself:

1. Have a few pre-digested 'thoughticals' in one-liners of the kind President Reagan used to write out on cue cards. They can be as simple as 'All Tories are bastards' or 'Labour would nationalise everything'. Something which encapsulates a mood but does not actually say anything is more effective than pages of cogent arguments.

2. Have a few figures ready to trot out. Do *not* say 'The figures cannot lie': every woman in the audience will resent it, and it is, after all, a politician's job to make them.

THE SELECTION

You are now in the lap of the gods - or, since these are all party members, sods. In Politics, unlike sex, the foreplay is not the most enjoyable part. The wisest advice is 'Lump it' - however badly you may be cheated, slandered or discriminated against.

There is no need for a closing speech. If you have lost, it will only make you look bad. If you have won, it is always best to be humble and inarticulate (for the last time!).

ELECTION

You can take this for granted. Backstabbers make sure they only get selected for safe seats. So treat the poll as a three-week outward bound course to test your powers of endurance and prove that you have the necessary qualifications for a political career: the constitution of an ox, and preferably the brains to match.

THE RULES OF THE GAME

Now you have your ticket to the great game of power. Not power itself - you will have to backstab much more to get that. Get into the game quickly and accelerate your progress by following these rules:

RULE 1 - Conceal the kind of bastard you really are: although it is taken for granted that you are one, it is counter-productive to show it. Westminster is a small, intimate system. Everyone's foibles and failings are common knowledge and wildly exaggerated.

RULE 2 - Know your enemies. In Westminster there are 649 of them. The other side is a generalised enemy - a straw man to attack. Genuine hatred and backstabbing should be reserved for the real threat - members of your own side. Parties are not the fraternal bands (or, in the Tory Party, the decent regiment) they would have us believe, but groups of competitors bound together by mutual loathing.

RULE 3 - Be absolutely clear about your aims and priorities: you first, and the party second. But always stick with the party, even if it is down: disasters bring new men to the top. YOU. In disaster, as Lenin said, there is always hope for some. Play parties like shares and only invest in one that is about to take off.

RULE 4 - The constituency is not a priority for Backstabber, merely his admission ticket. If your seat is marginal you will certainly have to work at it: be seen there every week, appear regularly in the local paper (although you can do that without bothering to go to the place) and on the local radio station (ditto, since the advent of the telephone). Above all, you will have to be nice to some unspeakable people - and *no* Backstabber wants to do that, or be at everyone's disposal like a real MP, to whom constituencies are the only true joy of Politics. Unless your seat is a marginal one, it is just the same as any other you would sit on. You do not have to keep looking at it, driving in new nails or polishing it. But if it is in danger of collapse, you had better find another to sit on.

MORE ADVICE ON CONSTITUENCY MATTERS

Constituencies are nymphomaniac: the more they get, the more they want. And if you let it, your constituency can drag you down into full-time social work, leaving you no time to get on with the real job of backstabbing in Parliament. To be branded as a 'good constituency MP' is to be labelled a failure - someone who poses no threat. So constituencies should be seen and not heard - and kept firmly in their place, which is miles away. Let your secretary run yours, while you take the credit. She is almost certainly far smarter than you and will do it for less money, while you get on with stabbing backs . . . everyone's, that is, except hers.

THE WESTMINSTER ARENA

In Politics, forget the old public school maxim 'It matters not who won or lost but how you played the game'. Politics is pointless if you don't win. Lose, and you are relegated forever to rare appearances in your constituency rag. Politics is neither art nor science, nor even a craft (though plenty is involved). It is surf-boarding. Most of the time, it is paddling. Occasionally, and usually unpredictably, it is seizing a wave to ride with it as far as you can, before transferring to another. The moves, moods and dynamics of Politics are neither right nor wrong, and you neither create nor control them - they are transport. Momentum is the only excitement (even if it is downhill). Grab opportunities as they come and use them without squeam or scruple. Try to be a sheep with the instincts of a barracuda.

Parliament is a free masonry - a club - a forum for that war of each versus the other called Politics, while protecting its Members against the world outside. Conform to the unwritten rules of the club: join the Parliamentary Masonic Lodge to ensure that the Whips, the clerks and many of the duller MP's and journalists will not try to knife you all of the time. Get yourself some comfortable niche in a firm with more money than sense, who will give you a few thousand a year and lots of trips abroad to act as their consultant on things they should know anyway. Be nice to secretaries and researchers: they will be so amazed that they will keep you up to date on all the lowdown. They know everything that goes on and will tell all for the price of a drink, the oil on which Westminster floats. Be sociable, but stay solitary: Politics is a lonely art, a bit like masturbation - you must never let it get out of hand.

Backstabber must compete. Virility displays are essential. You must quickly establish that you are as vicious as the rest. Practise strutting while sitting down, and snarling to defend your non-existent integrity. Once all that is established, stop and become charming. Parliament's reputation is B'stardly, but there is no need for *excessive* backstabbing. That just discredits everyone. And being too pushy is also counter-productive - *vide* Kilroy-Silk.

BACKSTABBER'S PLAYGROUND

If the Chamber of the Commons is Parliament's paediatric paradise, then that of the Lords is its geriatric ward - inhabited by practitioners whose intentions remain as malign as ever, even though their grip of the knife has become arthritic and senility prevents them remembering where to insert it (unless Lord Denning or another of his ilk goes berserk with knife, fork and spoon as well). The Zimmer frame may be a more natural weapon. The game in the Commons is played with tighter rules by professionals in their prime. Those who most want to stab you *and* their own front-benchers in the back, are seated behind both - in full view of the other side and the television cameras. So only the odd barb from an anonymous back-bencher, or a belated savaging from a long-dead sheep, ever finds its mark - and both end up as carcasses. In the Chamber, successful attacks *must* be full frontal.

Anyone who gets upset or hurt by being abused, attacked or

OUT OF SHOT, OUT OF ORDER

maligned is clearly unfit for Politics. It is a mercy to force them out and into a career to which they would be better suited, such as social work. Such bombardment is part of the necessary toughening-up process for politicians. Ultimately they will have to go out there and face Jeremy Paxman and a public whom they have let down, betrayed and lied to for decades when promising to make Britain a better place to live while things got steadily worse.

PATHWAYS TO POWER

Having got fit for real Politics by emotional drying-out, go on to refine your skills inside your own party. There are a number of options to choose from:

THE REBEL RUN - By this pathway came three of our greatest politicians - Winston Churchill, Harold Macmillan and Harold Wilson. Neil Kinnock rose this way too. The hypocrisy of parties means that they can only be led to the safety of the centre ground by a politician from the extremes. Time your rebel run with care. Wait until the leadership is failing, as it tries to implement the policies it developed in opposition and discredits itself in the process. Pursue the rebel run too long and too far, and it becomes a show biz gimmick - a life sentence of being Denis Skinner. It can even be fatal - like Tony Benn who immatured with age. Remember, leaders become paranoid ten minutes after election, and the politics of failure make paranoia a system of party management. Exploiting this characteristic by feeding it is far more sensible than confronting it.

THE BROWN NOSE - A much better bet. Conform to the mood of the moment, safe in the knowledge that as long as you do not go overboard or commit yourself up to the armpits, you can always climb out into another fashion as the first one fades. Nothing lasts in Politics except the politicians.

THE METEOR TAIL - A variant on the above. Attach yourself to a rising star and let him pull you up. Choose wisely, hang on his every word until you have built up sufficient momentum - then kick the ladder away.

THE SPECIALIST TRACK - Establish an expertise in a narrow area so impressive and formidable that no Prime Minister in his right mind can ignore it. This does not guarantee advancement, but at least your nuisance value will be recognised - and you might also pick up a few outside directorships as a result.

THE SOUND CHAP - The best image to have. Demonstrate 'bottom', never panic (you do not understand what the flap is about), and smoke a pipe (it makes you look wise). Denis Healey, Gordon Brown and Harold Wilson all had great 'bottom'. Behind his image of bluff Yorkshire common sense and integrity, Harold Wilson was nervy, duplicitous, cunning and paranoid. He was - and still is - a master of disguise, concealing his duplicity in clouds of smoke. Look solid (something difficult to avoid in Parliament's festival of food and drink).

Choose any of these pathways to power, but always stay within the party. If you venture outside it, are too clever on television or in the media, or attractive to the electorate, you will be damned for ever.

PROGRESS IN THE COMMONS

Achievement in the Commons is necessary only to strengthen your position within the party. Concentrate on it. Speak frequently in its committees and meetings: it is there that you will be judged. The PLP and the 1922 Committee are the real testing grounds. Speak up, speak early, and speak well - but not too often. Your aim is to establish a reputation as a strong speaker. Leave the boredom factor to Bob Cryer or Robin Maxwell-Hyslop or Robert MacLennan. Politics is the art of mobilising symbols and giving the impression you mean one thing when your are in fact saying something else. Don't promise to give your audience what they want - you can't deliver. But always let them think you can. The good Backstabber politician will add the extra bonus of making them feel pleased at being deceived.

THE UNIFORM

The best Backstabbers blend into the background like guerillas - it makes the combat safer. Never stand out. The uniform of Politics is a suit: wear it everywhere, with a sober tie (either the Law Society's or pseudo public school) always worn tight but never Windsor-knotted. Blow-dry your hair - or if you have none, Scargillise it. Wear a perpetual smile and a sensitive look. Never laugh - at least not loudly. Laugh and the world laughs at you. Cry and everyone wants to know why. Politicians, like prunes, are black-coated workers whom people believe make the going great.

WHERE TO BE SEEN

Anywhere in 'the Palace' other than the Commons Chamber. Labour Members prefer the tearoom, which resembles a re-creation of the station buffet in *Brief Encounter*, where they can digest stale pies and fresh gossip. Tories prefer the Smoking Room, where the old buffer brigade grunt at each other. Both parties dine in the Strangers' Dining Room with constituency officers, who should be entertained minimally. The Harcourt Room is for being seen with companions of the opposite sex who are sufficiently attractive to improve your image. Use the Members' Dining Room only when alone (it is expensive), but never the canteen - a place strictly for the mean and iron-stomached, where poison is spread by conversational top dressing: Tories sit at one end in suits, Labour at the other in shirt sleeves, and they all gossip about each other - the *only* subject of conversation which interests politicians.

Your personal assistants should also be seen about the place. You will need as many as you can afford. They do no research (leave that to the Library), but these moles dig up dirt on other MP's and tap it into the staff bush telegraph; they leave incriminating documents about others in photocopiers and circulate anything damaging they find there themselves, for the photocopier is Parliament's built-in spy. Use it to ruin people, as well as copies.

BACKSTABBER'S ASSISTANTS

Parliament is superficially gregarious, but essentially lonely. There is no-one you can trust, but plenty you can use. Most useful are the Whips - the Sergeant Majors of Politics, with their scintillating intelligence and culture (something they spell with a 'k'). Nominally to be obeyed, they are really to be exploited. Whips store the dirty linen, compile the indictment sheets and know where the bodies are buried. Informants wishing to add to their malevolent stock treat them as a confessional, ingratiating themselves by proffering any dope they have sneaked or snitched, retail or wholesale, true or false. Let them know who's been seen with whom, who said what about the Leader, and they will collect and pass on the information. Promotion and demotion are engineered by the Whips, and any good fiction writer can keep them happy indefinitely. Backstabber will use this conduit of misinformation to shop all his rivals. In Politics a man is guilty until proved innocent, and the Whips are the jury.

Second in usefulness is the Lobby - not a place, but a generic term for the journalists who hang around a Palace of Varieties where everyone is in fact the same. Anything you tell them will be used but not attributed (an invaluable bonus for Backstabber), so keep on friendly terms and relay everything - fact or fallacy - they do not distinguish between the two, but never trust them. The Lobby like to think of themselves as the sewer, not the sewage, but of course they are both.

The newest channel is the Sisterhood: women MP's who think as a clique but gossip as a claque. Feed them with facts about your own efforts to advance the cause of women, and to defeat the sexism, exploitative antics of sexual aggression of other Members. Unfortunately, women Members have to be talked to rather than at. They must not be touched, embraced or enfolded in the way you can in *tête-à-têtes* with chaps, particularly those from public schools who always respond affectionately. The women can't on principle: they live in a fishbowl and must prove themselves one of the boys. Yet properly (not man-) handled they are enormously useful. They kill as a pack.

PARTY CONFERENCES AND ACTIVITIES

Places to be seen and scenes to be avoided. Conferences are the refuge of failures who will never make it in Parliament. Establish your presence, while staying away, by having messages screened and announced for you all week. Alternatively, drop in for the day, run around everywhere and be photographed falling into the sea. Or best of all, pay a double to attend for the duration to talk to ordinary delegates and buy them huge quantities of drink - preferably on somebody else's room bill.

Never speak on policy. That changes every four years and you end up contradicting your own video tapes. Never misbehave. The days when Tom Driberg could bugger delegates under the pier and Anthony Eden seduce fine gals are long past. Feminism has rendered Conferences miserable, and in any case every moment is now televised. The lasting effect is to discredit the parties and exhaust the Members. Backstabber will avoid both these pitfalls, but will ensure his enemies escape neither and will employ any stratagem to stop them leaving before the last note of 'Auld Lang Syne'.

FIRST STEPS FIRST

Progress in Politics is a miserable grind. The first steps are the dreary ones: working as an errand boy (or Parliamentary Private Secretary), a public school fag (or Junior Minister), or a thug in the Whip's office. You will have to travel round the country finding facts no-one wants to know, and doing the fetching and carrying that Ministers are too important to do (or which carry no bonus of publicity). And you will have to act as gaoler in all-night sittings for even the most lunatic adjournment debates.

There is no point in grumbling, passing malicious information to the media about your boss, or being in any way disloyal - even while you are being used and abused by him. This process of humiliation is to test that you are fit for the greater humiliations of high office. You are dependent on your immediate superior, who has tabs on you, and probably tapes too. If he wants to drop you,

you are out. On the other hand, if he likes you and you are good to him, he might take you with him when he goes somewhere. Hang on, hang in. If there are no waves for your surf-boarding he can act as a power-boat or, perhaps, a tug.

UPWARD MOBILITY FOR THE JUNIOR MINISTER

No real Backstabber is content to stay a Junior Minister forever. So attract the eye of the Prime Minister. Go in for assiduous service, total loyalty, and a flat refusal to refer to him as 'that bastard' on radio, on the telephone, or in letters left in the photocopier. Draw yourself, your new career, your abilities and general wonderfulness to the attention of the Lobby. Praise their articles and always approach them *seriatim*, for you must never praise one journalist in front of another, or leak information to two together. They have to be hand-fed and given the same information exclusively. Drink regularly - but never to excess - in Annie's Bar, buying rounds liberally for the journalists who frequent it. Outside the Commons, maintain a high public profile, throwing yourself into any available publicity: cycle at the Transport Department, live as a beneficiary at the DSS, go fishing at the Ministry of Ag. and Fish., or parachute onto oil platforms at the Department of Energy. Action Man is a good approach. What is more, you will not have to say anything of significance. As a Junior Minister that would be dangerous.

WAITING FOR TAKE-OFF

Attend the Commons at every available opportunity. Bray your loyalty to the rafters. A little backstabbing while you wait will keep your hand in - although remember that it should be applied sparingly to anyone higher than yourself on your own side, and never to the Leader whom you cannot afford to stab - yet. Accept every invitation to appear on Wogan or the Jimmy Young Show: the questions are soft, the audience huge. This is a tantalising stage when everything depends on the bitch goddess Lady Luck, from whom political blessings flow.

THE POLITICAL STUNT MAN

THE CABINET

Patience will bring you to the apogee - the Cabinet or Shadow Cabinet - top of the party pyramid and the hot-house of the Backstabber's art. Publicly your hands are clasped as brothers. Privately, the knives are out. You are now a master of information, the only source of power in Politics. Collect it, store it - out-squirrel Tony Benn. Dangle choice morsels in front of greedy journalists. Leak surreptitiously against other Ministers. At the top there is no loyalty - only convenience. Restrict your real malevolence to immediate and limited objectives. Scatter-bombing serves no purpose, except to destroy your reputation. What you are doing unto others, others are almost certainly doing unto you. So do it better. And bring to the art form some of the finesse and charm so sadly lacking these days.

Achievement in your actual portfolio is not important. Glittering success could turn others against you, and may even induce the Prime Minister to see you as a threat. On the other hand, total failure does disqualify - particularly in the House of Commons, which tests Ministers to destruction. Every parliamentary session sees a new Minister butchered by the Rottweillers on the other side.

The best course is a happy medium and a clean nose. Take responsibility for all the errors of your Department, while making it clear they are nothing to do with you. Help all your fellow Ministers with their personal problems (and memorise the details). Be available and nice to backbenchers - speak at their dreary dinners: you are the master now but must show it by being a servant. Yet the aim now is not to *get on* but to *get out*. At a moment of your choosing.

PICK YOUR MOMENT

Cabinet is not for keeps: Politics must remain an interest, not an obsession. The question you must ask yourself is 'Do I really want to become Prime Minister?' To be PM demands supreme ability (though none has achieved it yet) plus an excessive lust for power (which could be better applied to money). Prime Ministers are miserable workaholics who get no fun, lots of blame and who come to believe that no-one is worthy to succeed them - so they stay on forever until thrown out.

To avoid this, do not consider the job, even if you are one of the identifiable front runners. Only one can win. Coming second is the penultimate political failure: look at Geoffrey Howe. Coming first is worse, for after a brief moment of glory all Prime Ministerships end in failure and discredit.

THE JACKPOT

Rather than biding his time and hanging on in there to make his bid for the top, the sensible Backstabber will know when to call it a day. Stay long enough to become recognisable, then merchandise your image before your shelf life and reputation run out. The Cabinet is not so much a goal as a springboard for reaching the big time. Wait for a suitable moment - preferably just before your party hits the skids. Escape and sell what is left of your soul to the highest bidder. Perhaps a peerage (which carries a pension of around 50p for every minute you spend in ermine-lined sheltered accommodation), several directorships and possibly a few Government appointments. Parliament looks after its own.

Staying in Politics is like a window cleaner who develops a sexual fetish for the ladder. Get out and be happy. The rewards are enormous - far greater and far more easily earned than remaining in Cabinet to scrabble for peanuts with master Backstabbers. These perks are never exposed because you are out of the public eye. There is no need to hang on to your wife, or be dragged down by the delinquent children whom you have neglected for too long. Retire to fun, money, mistresses, drugs, or even an ITV directorship. Anything. It is all respectable compared to Politics, which most people regard as a life of crime. You will be able to go back to your old friends and look them straight in the eye. But don't tell them you have been in Politics - just say you have been in prison. They'll be happier that way.

Politics is the Nigel Lawson stairway to the stars: the most effective way of merchandising limited ability for maximum reward. Which would you rather be? As rich as Nigel? Or as miserable as John Major or Michael Foot or any other PM who hit the top and found they didn't like it? When you finally retire from the game of Politics you can publish your life's work - your alibi-ography. Dish the dirt on all your mates. You may not have always wanted to stab your colleagues, but after a few years in Politics you certainly will. At a tenner a knife-thrust, you will make a million.

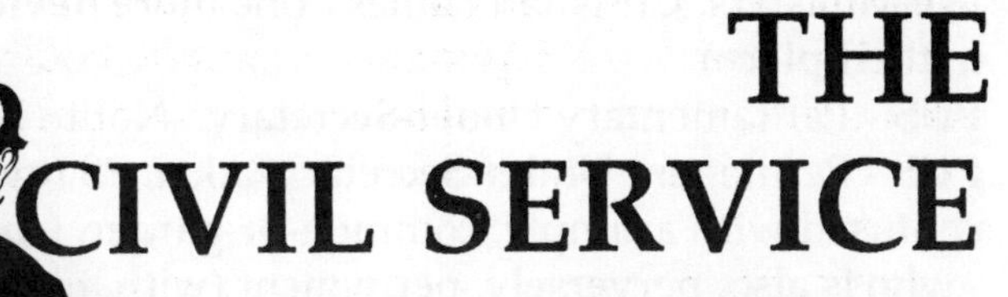

THE CIVIL SERVICE

by M.N. Darin

Certain hard-hearted cynics used to tell a joke about the Civil Service:

Q: Why are Civil Servants like the fountains in Trafalgar Square?
A: Because they play every day from ten to four

Forget it. Civil Servants have entered the fast and furious, round-the-clock world of running the country. They are not doing it for money. They are not doing it for position (how many Civil Servants admit to their job in public?). And let's face it, it is not likely that they are doing it for love either. So why do nice, ordinary - perhaps even mildly intelligent - people become Civil Servants? The answer is breathtakingly simple. They are doing it for POWER. Read on if you, too, want to end up telling 56,000,000 fellow Britons how to conduct their daily business.

SOME DEFINITIONS

Before you go further, you will need help with some of the more esoteric jargon of this grade-conscious world. Refer back as often as necessary to your personal introduction to Civil-Service-speak.

Minister - A minor functionary (obsolescent)
Cabinet Minister - Someone whose Christmas card looks good on your desk
Prime Minister - Deliberately referred to by the old fogey school

of die-hards as 'Marg-er-John'. (Incidentally, it is *very* swanky to use Ministers' Christian names - one more device for putting them in their place)
PUS - Parliamentary Under-Secretary. Not to be confused with -
PUS - Permanent Under-Secretary, a.k.a. PS (qv). Nor to be confused with a simple, common-or-garden Under-Secretary (qv) - who is also, perversely, permanent (with a small 'p')
PS - Private Secretary. A posh PS is PPS (qv) - or one of them, at least. But -
PS - Personal Secretary (a.k.a. Secretary - qv). A PS could be PS to a PS (qv), a PS (also qv) or possibly a PUS (ditto). This variety of posh PS is an SPS - that is, if (s)he is not a PPS (qv). Get it?
PPS - Principal Private Secretary. A highly eminent Civil Servant. But on the other hand, what about -
PPS - Parliamentary Private Secretary. A sort of very junior Minister - don't waste your time with this one
AS - Assistant Secretary. Comes under an Under-Secretary (qv)
US - Under-Secretary. Deputy to a Deputy Secretary (qv)
DS - Deputy Secretary. Really a Deputy PS (in the sense, that is, of **Permanent Under-Secretary** - that is to say, Permanent Secretary.)
Secretary -Secretary. Go back eight spaces. . .

If you can make sense of all that, you have already passed your qualifying test. And remember, rank is the very warp and weft of the Civil Service. But be warned, there are plenty more initials you will have to get your tongue round, and your first few months in the Ministry will feel like a total immersion course in gobbledygook. The aim, naturally, is to make the whole thing completely incomprehensible to the outsider. You may conclude that it all works pretty well.

STARTING POSITIONS

If you are serious about getting to the top in the Whitehall wonderland, there are a number of essentials you will need to get straight before you drop your application form (in triplicate, of course) into the postbox. For example:

Your sex - Try to be male if possible. (But if you insist on being female, see 'Women in the Civil Service' below.)

Your school - Contrary to popular belief, public schools are no longer considered *de rigueur*. Most Old Etonians nowadays seem to go straight into swilling Veuve Cliquot in the City, and some Civil Servants feel that they are not greatly missed. Nor does the sort of school to which the rest of us lesser mortals went cut much ice, either. You are in a quandary. Endeavour to ignore the problem. It will be good training for your future career.

Your university - A rather different matter - there are still considered to be only two of these. 'Redbrick', in Civil-Service-speak, means 'a good-natured chap who has been lying out on the beach for too long'.

Your accent - Don't have one - not at this stage anyway. Later on you will probably do well to fake some down-market vowels, to underline your egalitarian approach to life, if you are in that sort of job. But you must always be ready to swop straight back into BBC English.

ARE YOU PLAIN STUPID, OR WHAT?

Getting all these details straight will take you a long way. But the most important element, you will be told, is brainpower. After all, the brainpower of the British Civil Service got this country where it is today; and as it started, so must it go on - and on - and on.

Outsiders seem to be convinced that you have to be pretty short-changed in the brain department even to think of joining the Service. But you must be prepared to put on some sort of intellectual show to get in, if only to maintain the threadbare but gratifying fiction that Whitehall is the natural abode of the keenest brains in Britain. You will be letting the side down if you fail; and that is something that Civil Servants never never do. Not in public, anyway. Don't worry if you have not got two PhD's to your credit. A downright, barefaced lie about your academic qualifications might do the trick. Civil Servants may have designed your application form, but it is most unlikely they will read it once you have filled it in.

Later on in their careers Backstabbers may subtly hint at greater things, in true Civil Service style. So what if you attended Oxford Poly? You *were* at Oxford, weren't you? That will be sufficient to bluff your way through most conversations with your colleagues. This approach to dealing with your academic shortfalls is one you may apply successfully on many occasions throughout your career. You may find inspiration in the old *Times Crossword* trick. Your chums will be vastly impressed if you can - nonchalantly but publicly - fill in the grid in an ostentatious three minutes. Leave your office door wide open, slip your feet into their well-worn indents on your desk, and get to work on the back page. No-one will know that (Option A) you rose at 3 am and pored over the thing for four hours before getting into work; or (Option B - riskier but easier) you are writing complete garbage.

DRESS SENSE

Your dress is the next hurdle to clear. There is no longer any recognisable Whitehall stereotype. The bowler hat and rolled umbrella, beloved by cartoonists, went out a long time ago. So you will have to make up your own mind - something that does not come easily to a Civil Servant.

Wearing something a touch off-beam might stand you in good stead at your interview, but once you are in, your best bet is probably to wear whatever your boss wears. Imitation is, after all, the sincerest form of flattery. (If you are fussy about these things, check first that the boss is the same sex as you.) You may also consider wearing something a bit threadbare - it can help promote your image as someone above worldly considerations. It can even help your next pay claim. No need to wash your clothes too frequently, but rotating your shirts between airings can create an illusion of cleanliness if you are pernickety. And remember, no Civil Servant worth his salt ever cleans his shoes. But if you are so much as glimpsed wearing a pair of grey shoes you can forget promotion for at least ten years.

For further details on dress, as on so many delicate matters of Civil Service etiquette, refer to the excellent TV documentary series 'Yes, Minister'.

IMITATION IS THE SINCEREST FORM OF FLATTERY

A FOOT IN THE DOOR

There is a huge mythology about the selection procedures - polished tables the size of football pitches, serried ranks of misanthropic, superannuated old sadists, bright lights shining in the face - that sort of thing. It all started in the last century when a sanctimonious old killjoy decided to clear up corruption and patronage in the Service, and boringly insisted on entry by open public competition.

Don't worry about the gruesome tales of two-day-long IQ tests, and hidden cameras checking to see if you eat your peas with a knife. The selection procedures are entirely arbitrary and outside your control. (And don't worry, either, if at first you miss the Victorian corruption and patronage. That will come aplenty - once you are in!) Generally speaking, you will be all right at your interviews if you:

- agree with *everything* the interviewers tell you
- tell no jokes of any description *whatsoever*
- conceal the fact that you have put in job applications to thirty other potential employers
- subtly convey the impression that you think policy work on rape seed oil import quotas is both interesting and important.

More ambitious applicants - viz. Backstabber - will take the trouble to commit to memory a few sophisticated facts on current affairs: which Party is in power, whether or not we are at war - that sort of thing. But the truth is that you will probably be safe if you can even remember what day of the month it is.

START AS YOU MEAN TO GO ON

Once you have satisfied the selectors you will find yourself lodged in a nice, cosy Whitehall Department. Ninety-nine percent of Civil Servants work not in Whitehall but in what the remaining one percent refer to disdainfully as the 'real world'. But never forget that as a Backstabber you are professionally committed to ignoring all that 'real world' stuff. Henceforth, 'regional postings' and 'local offices' will be things of ridicule to you.

You will need to decide very quickly what particular job you should wangle for yourself. A great deal depends on it. Those bent on a knighthood before their 50th birthday must studiously avoid all contact with the less desirable nooks and crannies of their respective Departments of State. In particular, anything to do with such unsavoury aspects of public life as vehicle licensing, poor people, Ulan Bator, the North of England, incontinence, and the *Control of Toothbrush Manufacturing (Northern Ireland) Regulations* is best left to one side. Try instead to find a job which:

- will provide maximum exposure to Ministers

- will offer a decent quota of freebies (Backstabber will have a particular talent for appropriating these)
- will lead to a major public review of the policy in hand, followed by an inter-departmental Committee, a White Paper, high profile media attention, and early legislation
- will be swiftly forgotten once you have been rapidly promoted to a new job, and the policy has gone horribly wrong, leaving your unfortunate successor to rewrite everything from A to Z.

In this well-worn way, any cock-ups (or, in Civil-Service-speak, 'less successful decisions') will go unnoticed, your files will languish forever in some dusty storeroom, and your career will continue unblemished.

FEATHERING YOUR NEST

Before your feet are under - or more probably on - a suitable desk somewhere, you must target exactly which desk you want, and in what office it will stand. As a determined Backstabber, you will know instinctively that this choice will be as important as the job itself. Regular space standards are, in theory, a thing of the past. But you will still need to fight hard to ensure that you have more floor space than others of your grade. Such pettifogging one-upmanship is meat and drink to Backstabber, and you must take up the challenge at the earliest opportunity. Failing that, a thicker carpet than that to which your grade entitles you, or an extra window, can do wonders for your reputation. Remember, at least one Permanent Secretary-to-be consolidated his Departmental reputation for all time by smartly misappropriating a table lamp designated for a superior officer. So seize the opportunity of annexing any non-standard furniture if and when it comes your way. No-one will challenge you - possession is nine-tenths of the law in the jungle.

Another small tip: display some photographs of offspring around the office. (If you have none, produce some quickly. There may be nothing wrong with you, but the Civil Service prefers adherence to the norm.) The reaction of your colleagues will be a useful indication of their intentions towards you. Be suspicious of anyone who praises the children too lavishly - you are probably looking at another Backstabber. Likewise, be equally suspicious of anyone who ignores them - that is a *sure* sign the knife is out. You must be suspicious of absolutely everyone all of the time - or it could be *you* that gets framed.

BOSOM PALS

Throughout your professional career, you must pay the most scrupulous attention to who your friends are - something of a contradiction in terms for the genuine Backstabber. The basic rule is simple: *People with promotion prospects are always your friends.* Be he unpleasant or charming, domineering or amenable, lazy or hardworking - it makes no odds - latch mercilessly onto anyone who is, or might conceivably be, going places. Score bonus points by sucking up to those in higher grades, irrespective of who they are or whether they know you. Call them by their first name - a sure sign of a high flier - and do not be deterred if they cannot even remember you surname. Backstabber's skin is thick.

Sorting out those who are *not* your friends is just as important. You must learn to shun all inferior grades, all people with (genuine) regional accents, union members - anyone, in fact, who is unlikely to end up as one of the great and the good. Personal likes and dislikes have little place in the Civil Service rat race. The more unlikeable a person is, the more useful you are likely to find him. A painful philosophy, but it will pay dividends.

Other potential targets include: anyone who chats regularly to the Permanent Secretary, anyone who dines regularly with the Permanent Secretary, and anyone who *sleeps* regularly with the Permanent Secretary. All these people will be moving rapidly up the ladder, and you should do your best to ingratiate yourself with them.

Conversely, anyone who performs Gilbert and Sullivan in his spare time, anyone who takes part in the Departmental Sports Day (with the exception of the Permanent Secretary, who is there *ex officio* and has no choice), or anyone who is in - or indeed has heard of - the Computer Division, should be ruthlessly and publicly snubbed on all occasions. And see above for those tell-tale grey shoes . . . .

TROUGHING

Who you lunch with is not always the same thing as who you are friends with, but it is just as important. For the dynamic Backstabber Civil Servant, lunch is the lynch-pin of the working day. The winebars of Whitehall are thronged with threadbare pin-stripes from 12 to 3pm, and this is when the real business is conducted. If you are serious about your career, make sure you are highly visible every midday in the most fashionable local watering-hole. Cheap white wine is the staple liquid lunch. They say that you are what you eat - or, in this case, drink - so it should be obvious why so many Civil Servants are white, wet and mildly alcoholic.

Remember the old saw 'A blank lunch diary is a wasted opportunity'. Pluck up your courage, invite a Deputy Secretary or two to join you in a bottle of house white ('A Sancerre a day keeps promotion in play') and look forward to a couple of hours' congenial and productive backstabbing. No need to worry that you might be out of your conversational depth. These mandarin drones will not be debating alternative models of the national economy: they will be ridiculing their colleagues, checking through the list of those ahead of them on the promotional ladder, swapping notes on who is next in line for retirement, or notching up high scores in the never-ending games of 'Drop a Name', 'Who's Afraid of the Permanent Secretary?' and 'My Ego's Bigger Than Yours'. Remember, these are games that you too can play.

THE RIGHT IMPRESSION

Turn your attention next to your working habits. Consider your image carefully. Are you, for instance, turning up too early in the morning? This is normally considered *infra dig*, and although some clever people affect it without obvious detriment to their careers, there is no evidence that it pays. Far better - and easier - to breeze confidently into the office at 10 o'clock, - the clear implication being that you were there until after 8pm the night before. A fiction, naturally, but an impressive one.

Equally, you should make a frequent point of leaving work on the stroke of 5.30pm. This theory relies on your colleagues concluding that you are macho enough to handle any criticism about skiving. If you work in London (and where else would Backstabber be working?) there is the added bonus that people may think you are going to the opera - always a good point to score. However, you are warned not to be over-confident. You cannot afford to ignore entirely the daily chukka of 'I'm Not Going Home First' in which your more pedestrian competitors will indulge. Yet if you pick your opportunity carefully, you will be able to relax for several months on the strength of one late night at the office. Just make sure that *everyone* is fully aware you will be burning the midnight oil: you could ask if anyone knows where you could find a camp bed.

You should also take up the age-old trick of the 'bulging briefcase'. Old it may be, but it still works. Your workmates believe you are going home with six inches of the contents of your in-tray. You alone know that your case really contains the office copy of *Private Eye,* two 'Twix' wrappers and a second-hand Dick Francis. Of course, some of your rivals *will* be taking home three hours of meaty policy work. They are that sort of person - they actually *like* work. For them, a relaxing evening at home means snuggling up with the latest White Paper on the reform of the Scottish Social Security system. But Backstabber needs no such recourse.

WOMEN IN THE CIVIL SERVICE

'The Civil Service is an equal opportunities employer' - or, in plain English, 'If you are a woman, you've had it'.

Well, maybe that is a bit harsh. Women do have an easier time in Whitehall than in some of the other professions (the Church and the Army leap to mind). And many of those women are frighteningly good. Even more of them are plain frightening! But, put simply, if you wear a skirt (and this applies equally to *both* sexes) you will have to fight that much harder to reach the top. There are three basic role models for the Whitehall woman:

1. The academic, with pebble glasses, 'I eat people as stupid as

you for breakfast' type, with a four-figure IQ

2. The man-hunting, haute couture, 'Look how successfully I combine elegance and savoir-faire with talent and ambition' type, also with a four-figure IQ

3. The down-to-earth-mother, placidly competent, 'I can hold down a demanding full-time job and still bring up four clever children - they're *so* rewarding' type, with - you guessed it - a four-figure IQ

Choose whichever model best suits your own natural inclinations. But be prepared for a rough ride from the cohorts of sexist swine around you. And remember that however clever, however dedicated, however productive you are, for every Dame in the New Year's Honours List there are a Thousand and One Knights.

SEX

A short section. Sex and the Civil Service are not natural bedfellows. There are exceptions of course, although to cite examples would be libellous. And when it does happen, traditional views on gender can be safely disregarded (as certain well-documented episodes in the history of our security forces bear witness). But for the average male Civil Servant, sex during working hours means a hasty glance at Page 3, or standing close to the typist at the Christmas Party. For the average female, even more depressingly, it means the boring daily routine of avoiding roving hands during committee meetings. The accepted general philosophy dictates that, Backstabber or not, your mind should be on higher things. You may not like it, but your career will certainly benefit.

THE SEVEN DEADLY SINS

By now, you should have a pretty good idea of the ground rules for carving a successful career in Whitehall. But what happens next? How do you proceed with the job of actively backstabbing your way to the top?

Learn by *other people's* mistakes. Indeed, as a Backstabber you will undoubtedly find this the quickest - as well as the most enjoyable - way of progressing up the ladder. You should also note and beware the Seven Deadly Sins for the Civil Servant. They take on a special meaning in the world of the pin-stripe and the triplicate form. Your personal Whitehall definitions follow:

PRIDE - The number one sin. There is no room for pride in Backstabber's make-up. How could there be, if you have to admit to being a Civil Servant at drinks parties? Backstabber's route to the top requires public self-abasement and private low cunning at every turn. There is no level to which he would not stoop.

SLOTH - You may not have to slave at your desk - perish the thought - but backstabbing is a 24-hour-a-day job. Get on with it.

AVARICE - You must be joking! If you want to be a millionaire by the time you are 20, go and start an airline. Backstabber is always able to bide his time. Think of all those lovely directorships which will come your way after you retire on your handsome, inflation-proof state pension.

ANGER - If you want to make real progress, you will have to learn to take any amount of flak. Civil Servants have been taking it since the first Stonehenge Planning Bill bit the paleolithic dust. There will be no room for anger when your colleagues, your superiors, your Ministers, your rivals or (ugh!) the Press find fault, jugulate you, etc. etc. Your back will have to be very, very broad. But console yourself: when you reach the top of the pyramid you will have limitless opportunities to victimise all your detractors - the power will be yours. Backstabber, like an elephant, never forgets . . .

LUST - On lust, refer to previous section. Generally speaking, it gets you nowhere and is bound to end in tears. Backstabbers do not bother. Lust for power, however, is a different matter, and something to nurture tenderly at all stages.

GLUTTONY - Not the most serious sin. But remember - there is no such thing as a free lunch. If you spend all your lunch hours being entertained by tenth-rate trade associations, you are wasting valuable backstabbing time.

ENVY - Well, truth to tell, this is no sin for Backstabbers. On the contrary, your single, sole and unique motivating force will be the unadulterated envy of everyone above you - everyone who is more powerful and more illustrious than you are. Envy will be your motivation, your driving force, your very life-blood.

'UP, UP AND AWAY...'

Think, finally, to the day when you realise that you have done it at last. Your faultless backstabbing technique has propelled you upwards, like a dazzling meteor, through Assistant Secretaryships and Deputy Secretaryships, the commissions and committees - fuelled by a high-octane mixture of minutes, memoranda, Bills and briefs. Up in the pure thin air of the Civil Service stratosphere, only the highest of high fliers remain. You are one of them.

The knighthood proclaims it to the rest of the world, but to you it also means a host of gratifying extras. Government art collection pictures adorn the walls of your office; you have a car, a driver and a Private Secretary; Junior Ministers treat you with reverence and awe - their diaries are rearranged to accommodate you.

But the final truth dawns when you reflect upon your (perish the thought) work. Someone once described an expert as a person who knows more and more about less and less. If so, then a Civil Servant must be someone who knows less and less about more and more. And when you finally realise you know precisely nothing about absolutely everything - *then* you can be sure you have made it to the very top.

THE BAR

by Bigwig

The first thing to remember about Barristers is that they like the sound of their own voices. Never be afraid to talk about yourself and your cases - everyone does! It is a little like playing the trumpet in the school orchestra - you need a lot of wind, but everyone knows that you are there.

Those who are thinking of embarking on a career in this learned profession should practise - in front of a mirror if necessary - the gentle art of blowing their own trumpet. Start with a few simple exercises, just like opera singers: 'Me, me, me, me, me, me. . . ' Remember it must never be 'You, you, you, you . . . ', or even 'Tell me about yourself' - that is only for social workers!

STARTING OUT

An apprentice barrister is called a 'Pupil'. Each Pupil is assigned to a 'Pupil Master', and your first task will be to impress your 'Master' in whatever way you can. Good legs can be a great asset - if you are a girl - but otherwise you will have to resort to knowing the answers to tricky legal problems. This is difficult to do without appearing a 'swot'.

The most important thing a Pupil must be is indispensable. Therefore not only must you be able to take a good note in Court, where you sit demurely behind your Master, but you must also be able to fill the gap in the Chambers' cricket team, taking five wickets and saving the match, while remaining commendably modest about the whole affair. It is a difficult business - and in fact thinking about it, anyone who is capable of walking such a delicate tightrope should probably forget about the Bar - they would almost certainly be much better suited to Politics!

GETTING INTO CHAMBERS

Barristers work in groups called 'Chambers'. To start pretending to earn your living (for the benefit of prospective fathers-in-law) it is important to join a good set of Chambers. Junior members are normally recruited from the wealth of talent amongst their own Pupils (see above), however this is not always so. Here are some examples of the Backstabber's approach to getting 'taken on' (as it is known), - as opposed to 'taken in' (which is what some candidates try to do to some Chambers):

'NEPOTISM RULES O.K., UNCLE'

Family connections have always been used in the Law, and the Bar is no exception. If you are fortunate enough to have a close relative who is someone important - father or uncle, or nowadays of course, mother or aunt - this is a good start (begin with the House of Lords and work downwards). However, be warned this ruse can backfire. The fact that you are Sir Jasper Claptrappe QC MP's favourite nephew might not necessarily provide you with an automatic passport into his old Chambers: he may have been so disliked that members of Chambers will not favour your application, and you could be sent on your way to mumbled sounds of 'That's enough Claptrappe for any set of Chambers'.

THE 'EXCEPTIONALLY BRIGHT AND GIFTED' APPROACH

If you are the sort of person who wins scholarships as easily as sneezing, you may feel able to try breezing into Chambers on sheer ability - being au fait with all the latest cases, having wise and articulate opinions on all aspects of forensic life and generally being an all-round clever dick. On the other hand, if like most people your intellectual furniture is more MFI than Chippendale you can always try to bluff your way through with a few well-chosen phrases such as:

- 'On all fours with' - No, not a sex position but a way of saying that one case is very much like another; or
- 'Having a second bite at the cherry' (have you got sex on the brain?) - This refers to a variety of situations in which a dissatisfied litigant is attempting to do something his lawyers would prefer him not to achieve.
- Use as many 'Latin tags' - with which the Law is littered - as you dare (see later for fuller list).

'THE SOLICITOR'S GAMBIT'

First of all, be a Solicitor. Then state that you have seen the error of your ways and want to become a Barrister. This could be greeted with gasps of anguish from your partners if you have achieved some status in this side of the profession . . . . . or alternatively (human nature being what it is) sighs of relief. You then find a likely set of Chambers which you feel could benefit from the work your old firm will undoubtedly be sending you, and launch yourself brazenly at them. This approach can have very mixed results, but these days is certainly worth a try.

BUILDING A PRACTICE

This can be a little like climbing the North Face of the Eiger in your bedroom slippers. However there are certain ground rules which all Backstabbers will know by heart and use ruthlessly. Here are some of the more obvious ploys:

BUTTERING UP THE CLERK

Barristers' professional lives are run by their 'Clerks'. These are persons whose lack of formal qualifications in no way impedes the enormous influence they have, particularly over the emerging young Barrister - so be nice to your Clerk! In fact be very nice. Ask him whether he had a good day at the races (dogs, of course); he probably owns a greyhound or two, if not the entire stadium.

Always appear concerned if he is under the weather or even injured (quite possibly by some disgruntled senior member of Chambers!). And be prepared to go for a drink with him ('A swift half, Sir?' - that's him asking, not you) at the 'Dog and Duck' or the 'Greasy Mermaid', so as to steal a march on your rivals at the junior end of Chambers.

If your line in toadying pays off, you will find that the 'Briefs' (as cases are known) come flooding in. If, on the other hand, your Clerk is not quite as gullible as you thought - and many Clerks are not - then you will be seen as the snivelling little arse-licker that you are. Oh dear, back to the drawing-board - or possibly consider becoming a Barrister's Clerk yourself.

BUTTERING UP SOLICITORS

Solicitors come in all shapes and sizes, but the one thing they all have in common is that they are the prime providers of work for the Bar. They must therefore be treated not merely with deference and respect, but with positively sycophantic enthusiasm. For example, when speaking to a Solicitor on the telephone always begin with with some cheery, albeit quite insincere, remark: 'Ah, Mr Bloggs (or Cuthbert if you know him well enough - i.e. you have spoken to him once before), how nice to hear your voice.' This means that even though you cannot bear the sound of his voice you would like to hear it more often.

If you know that a Solicitor has a hobby - amateur operatics is a common one, but sailing or embroidery are not unknown - make sure you bring this subtly into the conversation. This will not only create the illusion that you are interested in him as an individual, but it will also prove a useful distraction from talking of the case that he has rung up about, - which of course you were just getting round to considering, having only had the papers for six months.

JARGON

The importance of this cannot be overstressed. The Law, like the medical profession, has its own words and phrases, many of them in Latin, which are designed to sound good as they roll off the tongue, while meaning next to nothing to the man in the street (or 'Client', as he is known!). The accomplished Backstabber will realise instinctively the importance of appearing one-up. The gentle art of 'Wigmanship' is greatly enhanced by the selective use of jargon. Here is a list of some material that might prove invaluable:

LATIN SECTION (NO, THIS IS NOT 'COME DANCING'

sine die (sigh-knee die-eh) The case has been adjourned until God knows when - hopefully I shall be on holiday
res ipsa loquitur (rays ip-sa lock-quitter) We really don't know how this accident happened but somebody must be to blame and anyway the Defendants are worth suing
mens rea (men's rear) Nothing to do with masculine backsides!
prima facie (prime-a fay-she) At first blush - be wary of saying this if you have been drinking: you could sound totally plastered!
bona fide (bone-a fie-day) Not something that Mrs Barbara Woodhouse says to her dogs, but someone who acts in good faith - not readily applicable to Backstabbers

GENERAL SECTION

'This case will turn on the evidence' (I haven't a clue who will win)
'Providing the witness comes up to proof' (Nothing to do with the witness being drunk, more a hope that he says what he is supposed to say)
'As surely as night follows day such and such will happen' (Well, it might happen)
'Taking all the circumstances of the case into account' (This is a bit like playing 'Pin the Tail on the Donkey')
'He who comes to Equity must come with clean hands' (Nothing to do with grubby actors, but something which Chancery Barristers trot out when the going gets tough)

COURT SECTION (FOR USE IN FRONT OF JUDGES)

'I'm much obliged to Your Lordship' (Thank you so much for asking my client the one question that has completely scuppered the entire case)
'With respect to my Learned Friend' (The silly fool is wrong again)
'May it please Your Honour' (. . . and it's more than likely that it won't)
'In my limited experience in this field' (I know everything there is to know)
'May I be of some assistance . . . ' (It is highly unlikely that you can be, but it never hurts to sound helpful)

HOW TO BE A BUSY JUNIOR

Barristers who have not yet 'taken Silk' (see later) are known rather quaintly as 'Juniors' - even if they are well into their eighties and possess none of their own teeth. They are instructed to do the run-of-the-mill cases. To be successful you must always appear busy, even if you are not. The successful Backstabber must observe a few rules to maintain this illusion:

1. Never take your holidays in vacation time (when all the other Barristers are sunning themselves in the South of France). Be around so that you will pick up some good 'Returns' (as cases originally sent to other Barristers are called). You can then slip away quietly at the busier times of year and so give the impression that you work much harder than you do.

2. Always make the case you are doing sound very important. Phrases such as 'international ramifications' should be employed even when you are defending a simple shop-lifter. The fact that the only 'international' aspect involved was the name of the store concerned should not be stressed!

3. Subtle name-dropping is also an art to be studied. Refer

nonchalantly to your House of Lords case which has had to be adjourned again. There is always a very big building case just around the corner that will take you to Hong Kong for several months. And as for the European Court of Human Rights - well, they are just begging to hear your every word (translated simultaneously into sixteen languages). But the seasoned Backstabber will take great care not to overdo these references as there is always a danger of getting caught out. If you do happen to run into someone who is going to rumble you - like a member of the Court before which you are claiming to be appearing - don't panic. Remember, act natural, change the subject and - as they say - Never explain and never apologise.

4. Remember that Barristers are always supposed to know the answer. Being nonplussed or taken aback is not something that should be seen - certainly not in the successful Backstabber Barrister. When in Court you receive totally the wrong answer from a witness - generally your own client - show no sign of emotion and greet the devastating remark with a confident 'Exactly!', as if this was part of your case all along.

5. When the Judge, looking puzzled, peers at you over his half-moon spectacles (regulation issue to the Judiciary) and enquires quizzically: 'Surely, Mr Backstabber, you are going to refer to the rule in the case "Jones vs. Bloggs" ', you come back with a confident 'Your Lordship is, as always, ahead of me. I was just coming to that very point' (the fact that it had completely eluded you is neither here nor there).

6. If Fate looks kindly upon you - and you have followed some of the basics - then your practice as a 'busy Junior' should develop so that one case follows another in quick succession. Indeed you may become so busy that it is difficult to remember which case you are doing. Try not to get them muddled up. A man charged with handling stolen property may take justifiable offence if in conference with him you ask about the 'murder weapon'. A common tactic when you have been rushed into a conference for which you have not had all the time in the world to consider the

papers (i.e. you haven't read them), is to beam at your client in an urbane fashion and say: 'Now, Mr Jones (reading his name surreptitiously from the outside of the Brief), this is a very interesting case. Why don't you tell me about it in your own words.'. Hopefully, like so many things in life, all will become clear in the fullness of time. Anyway, until it does keep your fingers crossed and listen intently.

7. The Bar is all about competition, and you are mainly in competition with other members of your Chambers. The successful Backstabber must always steal a march on his rivals. In general terms this means getting the case before others. Some of the ways of staying ahead of the field are set out above. If all else fails I suppose you will have to resort to pushing your competitors under a taxi as they cross Fleet Street to get to the Royal Court of Justice ('over the road' as it is known in the Temple). This method is unsubtle and can result in your being charged with Attempted Murder, which may be something of a set-back.

8. Sometimes, however, there are cases that you are not keen to do. The technique here is to have a long conference with the client, extolling the virtues of his rather borderline case. Conclude the conference with a spirited exhortation: 'Well, Mr X, I am sure we shall be successful, indeed I'll hang my wig up if we fail.' The client leaves flushed with a feeling of confidence. You then deftly 'return' the case to your rival, who promptly loses it. The client is mortified, but of course thinks 'If only Mr Backstabber had done the case it would have been different.' (15 : Love to Backstabber!)

9. Likewise you must be on your guard against becoming the victim of your rival's similar ruse. If you find yourself in such a position - the late return of a fairly hopeless case - meet the situation with your customary panache: 'Of course the Law has changed since Mr Rival advised you so carefully'; or: 'I think Mr Rival might have taken a different view had he known about . . . ' (then refer to something which Rival certainly knew all about but make it sound as though he didn't). Use any number of the jargon

phrases set out above. However the best counter-ruse is to avoid getting the Return in the first place.

TAKING SILK

Barristers who have shown that they are erudite, competent, accomplished and in the right place at the right time, may apply to the Lord Chancellor to become a 'Silk'. If your application is successful you will be referred to a Leading Counsel and be entitled to the letters 'QC' after your name. This stands for 'Queen's Counsel' and not for 'Quite Conceited' - although in certain cases this is an easy mistake to make.

As a Silk, of course, you only appear in Big Cases: your clients are either big multinational conglomerates or murderers (you must learn to tell the difference). Generally you appear with another Barrister (on the same side) who is your Junior (see above under 'Busy Junior'). You are referred to as 'The Leader' or 'My Leader' by your deferential Junior. You courteously refer to your Junior as 'My Learned Junior', particularly when you want to rely on the very keen note that he or she has been taking of the proceedings - in the hope that it will substantiate your latest breathtaking 'Submission' (as arguments in Court are referred to - nothing to do with all-in wrestling, although with certain Judges the similarity can be terrifyingly close). Try not to appear too vexed when an inspection of your Learned Junior's note reveals only a few scant jottings and his tips for the 2.30 at Newmarket. Remember panache is the name of the game. A confident 'Just as I thought!' as you adroitly move on to the next submission will save the day.

The Backstabber in Silk is really just the same creature as the backstabbing Junior Barrister and many of the same aids can be exploited. You have, however, got the advantage of being able to use your Junior as an added ploy. Try to organise a bright swot-like individual (not, obviously, the laid-back devotee of the turf referred to in the last example). Get the backroom genius to tackle all the tricky legal research, prepare the appropriate schedules and to do as much spadework as an Irish navvy on double-time. Then you may confidently sail into the 'Consultation' (as a meeting with the Client is now rather grandly called) safe in the knowledge that you have all the answers at your fingertips.

QC's never hurry. There are always those around to do the bustling, the fetching and carrying, and the going to get things. The story is often told of the famous Silk, Edward Marshall-Hall, now long dead, who was always preceded into Court by his Clerk who carried his rubber cushion, his Solicitor who carried his papers, and his Junior who carried his medicines. Finally, just as the case was about to start, the Great Man would sweep in theatrically. Apparently he was also in the habit of blowing the rubber cushion up noisily while his opponent was telling the jury about some serious part of the case. Today rubber cushions in Court tend to be frowned upon. I suppose the modern equivalent is the digital watch alarm. But not even Backstabber QC has to descend that low - he can rely on much more subtle tricks of the trade. All these he will do gracefully and in his own good - highly-paid - time.

INNS OF COURT

There are four of these:- the Inner and Middle Temples (which sound like something on a darts board), Lincoln's Inn and Gray's Inn. They are all referred to with great reverence as 'The Honourable Society of . . .', and all Barristers have to belong to one. To recommend any one of these as the best for the budding Backstabber to join is rather to miss the point. The successful Backstabber will do equally well at any Inn. Once again it is all a question of following a few basic ground rules:

EATING DINNERS

All new members of the Inn have to eat their dinners (just like Nanny always said). Indeed before anyone can become a Barrister, or be 'called to the Bar' as it is known, they have to keep so many terms and eat so many dinners. These are usually quite jolly and reasonably sumptuous affairs. As the wine circulates and the port is passed, it is easy to feel that you have made the right decision in coming to the Bar. However try not to get too plastered - throwing up in front of the 'Benchers' (as the senior members of the Inns are called) is not on the whole a passport to preferment. It is one thing to be called to the Bar; it is quite another to be under it!

CALLED TO THE BAR, NOT UNDER IT

THE COMMITTEE MAN

As a student member of the Inn, the embryonic Backstabber will try to get onto the committees of as many organisations as possible. All Inns have a selection of student societies and debating societies. Remember, don't be shy - always seek the limelight. Once a Barrister, the rules do not change: continue to put yourself forward as a useful member of the Inn. Volunteer to run the glee club, if there is one; and provide the entertainment for the annual ball - or at the very least get on the ball committee. With luck this will bring you to the attention of those that matter, ahead of your rival.

Finally, always go in for any sporting activities organised by the Inn. Croquet is always a favourite. It is not too strenuous, and it is delightfully savage in that you can have the satisfaction of sending your rival's ball hurtling across the croquet lawn, while your partner - an eminent Lord Justice - looks on in admiration. A word of warning: do not underestimate some players who may look mild and inoffensive - they probably play for England in their spare time.

If, therefore, you manage to keep to the basic ground rules - be nice to all those who matter, get on the right committees, be in the right place at the right time, and account well for yourself in the croquet championship - you will probably be a great success and become a prominent and well-loved member of your Inn. In due course, as you age gracefully and grow in prominence and prosperity, you may even become a Bencher and be able to sit at the High Table with the great and the good. A just reward for any Backstabber.

A FINAL WORD

A certain mystique and glamour surrounds Barristers in the outside world. The Backstabber will be fully aware of this and, again, use it to his advantage. When applying to join the local golf club the fact that you are a Barrister may give you the edge over, say, the local artificial inseminator - or Livestock Officer, as he will probably want to be called. Although this may depend on the club: if you say rather grandly 'I'm at the Bar' in the wrong sort of club you may end up paying for the next round of drinks!

Many people like to invite Barristers to dinner, fondly thinking they will be witty and amusing. Try to preserve this illusion. There is nothing more disastrous for a hostess than to find that her star guest has bored everyone rigid during the evening with a monologue about the *Toad Sexing (Miscellaneous Provisions) Act* on which he considers he is something of an authority. People will want to hear about your salacious cases. Don't disappoint them. If in doubt make something up - after all, spinning stories should be second nature to you. The accomplished Backstabber should have no difficulty: available for dinner parties, bar mitzvahs and supermarket openings - just telephone my Clerk for an appointment.

See you in Court.

Backstabber

THE POLICE

by Brian Hilliard

There is still an old-fashioned notion that the way to the top in the Police Service is to arrest more people than anyone else. There are even some Police Officers who believe this. Nothing could be further from the truth. Arresting people attracts the risk of a complaint, and arresting a lot of people attracts a lot of complaints. So even before you join, jettison this arresting idea. You will be the better for it, you will have more time to dedicate to your backstabbing career, and you will gain a reputation as a courteous officer who gets on well with the community. It is essential, if you want to make any sort of progress, to refer constantly to 'the community'. It follows that it is equally essential that you ensure that anyone standing in your way earns a reputation as one who ignores the wishes of 'the community'. But one thing at a time.

For those of you who have ever heard a senior officer speaking on television and thought 'How on earth did he get that job? I could do it with my eyes closed' (a very effective way to police certain areas) - the first problem will be joining the Force. It is not enough simply to be over 172cms (yes, the Police are metric as well) with a newish pair of boots: you need a gimmick. A degree in computer studies is best (although a rugger Blue is just as acceptable in certain Forces); a family in the licensing trade is also a good start. There are plenty of oiks with four GCSE's and 20/20 eyesight to fill the rank and file: the potential Police Backstabber will make sure he has something extra to offer that sets him apart from his rivals from the outset.

AT POLICE TRAINING SCHOOL

All training schools have bars. Quickly ascertain the drinking preferences of each instructor, and make sure he knows you are buying. The training school is also the ideal place to acquire the most basic requirement for any career-minded officer: you must learn to hold your drink, and to establish an iron control over your intake. Wily Backstabber will very soon hoist aboard the infinitely variable range of opportunities which will be presented in each rank to dispose of rivals with drink-related problems.

Apart from that, keep your buttons polished, familiarise yourself with the *Construction and Use Regulations*, and you will be on your way. Watch out, however, for the committed swot who is determined to take the baton of honour at the passing-out parade. Unless you act promptly, this person will keep popping up during your career, hoping to be promoted in your place. So now is the best time to remove him or her. It will never be beyond the wit of the born Backstabber to arrange for such a rival to be found in bed (preferably with a person of the same sex) during the training period. If the upstart is inconveniently chaste, slip a packet of hash into his locker then denounce him (with a show of obvious reluctance). If the upstart is female, paper the wall of her bedroom with pictures of naked women. Training school staff are very keen on heterosexuality: they will give the hapless lady a hard time and she will leave. Be careful not to pass-out too near the top of the class: this could antagonise the first Chief Superintendent you meet in the outside world who did not graduate so well himself.

ON THE BEAT

This is the most physically dangerous period of your career. Backstabber will naturally avoid pub fights, rowdy demonstrations, and any risk of coming face to face with a burglar. Your natural cunning will ensure that you fill your quotas by arresting harmless drunks and issuing fixed penalty tickets (this enables you to show that you have summonsed the requisite number of motorists - without having to speak to any of them). You would also be wise to avoid arresting the owners of dogs who foul the pavement: the Duty Sergeant may send you back to the scene of the crime to collect the evidence.

Now you have to make some strategic career moves, which will require a great deal of artful dexterity. This part is a real minefield for the unwary: you could easily make the wrong choice. The Police Service - or that part of which which offers the best opportunities to the committed Backstabber - is made up of little empires: departments which guarantee advancement, but which go in and out of favour as often as fashion dictates changes in the length of women's skirts. For three or four years, the place to be may be Community Relations; then the spotlight switches to Research and Development, or Management Services, or Forward Planning. The servants of these various masters are quickly promoted, and the wisest and most perspicacious accurately fix upon the Department most likely to become the next flavour of the year and arrange a transfer into it.

There is another way. There exist some Departments about which nothing is ever heard, but which can be just as profitable. The Annual Report Office, for instance, spends six months at the beginning of each year rearranging the statistics for the previous year, and then another six months collecting statistics to rearrange for the following year. This can be a very useful springboard, because most Chief Constables do not like what the statistics tell them, and anyone who is capable of rearranging them more favourably is assured of advancement ('An extensive refurbishing programme has been initiated' reads better than 'The Chief has spent £5,000 on a Jacuzzi for his Headquarters suite').

If you were wise enough to join with a degree in computer sciences (of course, you could lie about it: no-one will ever check up) your path is clear. Police Forces spend a great deal of money on computers without being absolutely certain just what the equipment does. If you put yourself forward as an expert, you will immediately move sideways and spend the early part of your career being taken out to expensive lunches by computer salesmen anxious to flog off their current hardware before the new versions clear Customs. You will also be in a position to mention confidentially to the officer in charge of computer development that Smith and Jones have been conning him for some time about the extent of their expertise: blame them for the increasing number of faults in the system (a few of which you can surreptitiously introduce yourself) and suggest that it might be sensible to transfer them forthwith. As he is unlikely to know anything at all, he will take your advice.

There is a school of backstabbing which favours advancement through sport. While it is true that rugger players, in particular, are kept off the streets so that they will be in top form for the weekend, sporting Backstabbers do run the risk of injury on the field. The choice is yours - unless you are a lady. Female Police sport, even at an international level, does not enjoy a very high status. And in both male and female events, the tiresome business of 'team spirit' and *'esprit de corps'* does tend to make things rather complicated for Backstabber.

BIG, BUTCH AND KEPT OFF THE BEAT

POLICE SPOKESMANESE

Before you can make the rapid progress in the Force that you deserve, you will need to master the art of being a Police Spokesman. The training school will have issued you with a great deal of advice for use on those occasions when you are called upon to speak on television or radio (like 'Stand still' and 'Don't mumble'). But if you are to succeed and can maximise these media opportunities to further your career, a bit more guidance is called for. Take the case of the Murder in Sidmouth Road:

'Police were called to a house in Sidmouth Road in the early hours of the morning. Officers are still at the scene and a statement will be issued later.' (The Detective Chief Superintendent in charge of the investigation has only just sobered up. It will be another two hours before he's fit to speak to the press.)
'A body was found at the scene. Foul play is suspected.' (The head is missing; so is the husband.)
'We expect an early arrest . . . ' (You'll be lucky. No-one's seen the husband for two months.)
'As the result of diligent Police inquiries, a man to whom we wished to speak is now in Police custody and is helping us with our inquiries.' (The husband came to the station with his solicitor. He has a cast-iron alibi for the time of the murder: he was on a sailing holiday with the Town Clerk)
'A man has been charged with the murder and will appear in court in the morning.' (Hope to Christ it *was* the husband. The Detective Chief Superintendent's drunk again and refuses to look for anyone else.)
'It has never been Police policy to comment on a decision by the court.' (It must be the first time in history that a Magistrate has thrown out a murder charge, awarded costs against the Police, and advised a defendant to sue for damages.)
'Detective Chief Superintendent Brown's retirement on grounds of ill health is not in any way related to the recent case the the City Magistrate's court which attracted such undeserved publicity in the national press.' (We stuck a pen in his hand when he was still

drunk and got him to sign.)
'As the result of further diligent inquiries, Police are now looking for another man.' (Two children found the head in a bin, wrapped in a newspaper, with the boyfriend's address on it.)
'A man is helping Police with their inquiries.' (Where have I heard that before?)

PROMOTION

Unfortunately, however devious - or even good - you may be, there is no way of avoiding the examinations for promotion to Sergeant and Inspector. You may have the good fortune to be one of those people who has no trouble absorbing facts about the maximum unladen weight of an agricultural vehicle used on roads with a speed limit of 40mph, or the circumstances under which a person who plucks daisies from a roadside may be arrested: for these lucky people the examinations are a walk-over. For everyone else it is a boring but necessary slog. Unless,that is, you are in a large Force with a computerised personnel record, in which case you arrange to have your details entered on the database as having passed the examination, then the next time a promotion opportunity comes up your name will automatically be displayed at the top of the candidate list.

SELECTION BOARDS

It will not be enough to have passed the examination for each rank; you must then convince a Selection Board that you are the ideal candidate. (Selection Boards go on all through your career, so we will spend some time on this procedure.) All Backstabbers will realise that no member of a Police Selection Board has received any formal training. They have a standard set of questions to ask, and a standard set of acceptable replies. The Chairman will run through the candidate's career. Number Two will be a hatchet man, whose objective is to make the candidate lose his temper. Number Three will appear to be sympathetic and hope to lead the candidate into indiscretion. They are putty in the hands of the true Backstabber.

Backstabber will have equipped himself with the full details of some scandalous episode in the past of at least one member of the Board, but must first undermine the confidence of his fellow candidates. Rule one, is to be first to arrive at the venue where the Board is being held. Some Forces warn all candidates to be there at the same time, others want them to appear at half-hour intervals. Either way, *you* be there early. When the next candidate appears, tell him you have just heard that the Board is very keen on the recent changes in the Codes of Practice. As no-one can deal with questions on the Codes without a handbook, the candidate will be thrown into a panic. You might also hint that the Board is said to be prejudiced against the Northern Division (where you happen to know the candidate is serving), and really wants to promote a black woman to demonstrate its commitment to Equal Opportunities. Variations on these themes can be practised on other candidates as they arrive.

Once you have been before the Board yourself, you will be in an even better position to shake the confidence of those still waiting to go in, with casual comments like 'Very routine. They've obviously made up their minds already', or 'Don't answer immediately - they had a go at me for my snap responses', or alternatively 'Impatient buggers - if you don't answer immediately they think you don't know and move onto the next question'.

Backstabber's own interview should be plain sailing. The Chairman's third question will be about your current posting. The question should be met by a puzzled silence. The Chairman will repeat it. You then reply - still looking puzzled - 'I do beg your pardon. You're obviously using the Johnson-Templar Selection Process. I thought the Chief disapproved of it. Awfully sorry, obviously my mistake. So you want to know something about my current posting . . . '. You have now emptied a whole barrel of red herrings over the Board. The Chairman will wonder if the other two knew that the Johnson-Templar Process had been discredited. The other two, naturally, have never heard of Johnson-Templar, but are not going to let anyone know that. And all three of them are shaken to their foundations by the implication that you know more about the Chief's feelings than they do themselves.

The next step is to hit them while they are still reeling. Throw in a quick reference to the scandal on which you briefed yourself beforehand: 'Of course, one of my concerns is to prevent these unfortunate liaisons between WPC's and married officers that lower a station's morale'. The one Board member who is currently right in the middle of such an affair will be terrified that any further questions will identify him. While the other two, who will quite probably have been guilty of similar indiscretions, will not want you to enlarge on the theme either. But as you have clearly indicated that you know more than is comfortable for them in your present position, the solution must be to promote you rapidly so that you move elsewhere.

This tactic can be especially useful when you are being interviewed by local councillors for appointment as Assistant Chief Constable and above. Councillors frequently have scandalous backgrounds, to say nothing of numerous political rivals who are only too willing to pass on the details. Rapid promotions and frequent moves can mean that you get a reputation for being a career butterfly - someone who flits from place to place; or a seagull - if you leave a nasty mess behind. Either way, it is a small price to pay for your meteoric rise.

FUN AND FREEMASONRY

Let us now turn our attention to sex, drink and Freemasonry. The fully-fledged Backstabber must be qualified in each. Freemasonry is obvious. There is a lot of it about, and since Freemasons promote each other, and get one another out of trouble, no self-respecting Backstabber would pass up such a ready-made opportunity. Unless you are female, or black, or a member of the Catholic Police Guild, at some point in your career someone will invite you to become a Mason. Masons like to have Policemen in their Lodges, especially if the Lodge has a preponderance of professional criminals - it makes for a healthy balance. Added to which, the Masonic Backstabber will have instant support for backstabbing all those non-Masons. But it will not always be an automatic choice: you could find yourself in one of those progressive Forces where only half the senior officers are Masons, and the non-Masons are more proficient at backstabbing than their bare-chested brothers.

As for sex and alcohol, it has been demonstrated at the beginning that a prudent mastery of the demon drink is a positive asset for aspirants to promotion. The ability to remain standing after the Annual Dinner Dance, after the congratulatory drink for those selected for promotion, after the wake for those rejected, after the piss-up because it's been two weeks since the last piss-up - this ability will enable you quickly to suss out who is having it off with whom. Which brings us to sex.

There are two traditional attitudes in the Police Service. One tolerates drunkenness and frowns on sex, while the other despises the drunk but turns a blind eye to philandering. Lucky indeed the Backstabber who finds himself at a station which permits both drinking and bonking. In such cases Backstabber will do well to invest in a video camera, which will provide enough material for two or three rapid promotions. There is one Deputy Chief Constable who owes his present appointment solely to the record he kept of a mixed outing to Goodwood Races. His coverage of the historic (if clumsily managed) exchange of WPC Blank's knickers with Superintendent Dash's jockey shorts, and his 50-second take of Chief Inspector Blot's theft of a bottle of whisky while the barman was helping the CID typist to unfasten the buttons on her blouse, propelled him through three departments and two ranks. An eventual judicious screening of part of the video to selected members of the Police Committee rubber-stamped his appointment to Deputy without the formality of an interview.

'MAY THE FORCE BE WITH YOU'

Once you have knifed your way to the top, you might think there would be little further need or use for your backstabbing talents. However, it always pays to keep your hand in, as you may well want to move onto a larger Force where there are more officers to whom you can delegate your responsibilities. Backstabbing at the Home Office can be tricky: most of the principals in that establishment have been using your methods for years, and can see another Backstabber coming at 100 yards in a fog. The same applies to the senior council officials with whom you will meet to arrange budgets, to decide who gets a Jaguar, and to work out how many trips abroad you can wangle without the local press becoming curious.

You can save your *piéce de resistance* for your retirement. Your memoirs can ruin the reputation of any serving officer against whom you hold a grudge and, written carefully, can deny him any chance of reply: 'Willis was perfectly adequate as an Inspector, but appointment to Assistant Chief Constable severely overstretched him. I think he suffered from a permanent nervous breakdown without having the courage to admit it.'

There. You've got the idea now. Off you go. Just bung in the application form, and you're away. And remember, none of this 'arresting' nonsense. You don't want to spoil a perfectly good career by doing what you are paid for.

THE CITY

by Jason Nissé

'You see, old chap,' said the Hon Peregrine Crookes-Arntwe, head of corporate finance at the merchant bank, Von Ribbentrop McAlister & Co., and arch Backstabber, over a fourth virgin Mary at 'Bootlicks', his afternoon drinking club, 'Backstabbing in the City is not so much an art form, or even a way of life, as an ingrained part of expected behaviour. One is so much expected to stab people in the back that conventional backstabbing is not only disingenuous, it is ineffective. Just as one is about to thrust the bayonet into the spinal column, one finds oneself double-stiletto'ed - one jab just behind the wedding tackle - by some northern oik with a degree in chemistry in league with a Euro-Yank who knows how to say 'syndicated convertible facility' in fourteen different languages . . . including Scottish.'

He leaned back, and fingered the understated South African gold tiepin which subtly failed to attach the front half of his Hermes tie to the back. 'You do not stab a man's back to achieve,' Perry continued, 'You stab it to survive. And as you proceed up the greasy pole, it is all laid in front of you: a directorship of a major public company; a safe Tory seat in the Shires, if you can stomach the plebs; the ear of the Prime Minister and the Governor of the Bank of England; a knighthood, - maybe even a peerage. But if you're shafted you end up working a 14-hour day for a 5-figure pittance and a Vauxhall Cavalier. That is, if you don't chuck it all in and find a job in industry - or worse, public relations.'

After three more virgin Mary's, and even a drink containing

alchohol, the arch Backstabber agreed to divulge the accumulated wisdom of 25 years of shafting competitors, clients and colleagues alike in the City. His conditions were strict: a large (undisclosed) sum of money to be placed in a Paraguayan bank account (the Swiss are too loose-tongued now that they co-operate with Interpol), a harem of young boys to be made available at a suitably discreet location within five minutes of his office, a non-executive directorship of the publishing company that prints this book, and complete anonymity. So herewith . . . .

THE PIERS BEST-BUGGAH (NAME CHANGED) GUIDE TO CITY BACKSTABBING

MARKETS

The City has a whole series of markets in which to lose fortunes. The good Backstabber will probably be familiar with the intricacies of each of them, but this is not essential.

EQUITIES - Shares, in real English. These should give investors some control over how the company is run, pay a dividend and be worth something. However, the advent of non-voting shares (those not owned by the management), investing for the future (cancelling the dividend), and accounting standards akin to the service on British Rail, have changed all this. Professionals call these pieces of paper 'risk capital'.

GILTS - Bonds that used to be issued by the Government before the Conservatives came to power.

EUROBONDS - A complex market in which giant Scandinavian companies that you have never heard of can raise money from dentists in Belgium. Somehow both sides seem to get a raw deal - which may be not unconnected to large numbers of young men in braces who drive Porsches around London. The market has a credit rating system run by agencies whose names include such key words as 'moody', 'standard' and 'poor'. The lowest rating normally given is three B's (which in real life is enough to get you into quite a good university!).

FUTURES - Buying something now for delivery in the future - rather like ordering a sofa (except that in the latter case there is some assurance you will receive what you ordered, and in the right colour). There are also things called 'index futures', where you buy something that does not exist now, will not exist in the future, and could not be delivered to you even if you wanted it to be.

OPTIONS - Buying the right to buy or sell something in the future. If you do not understand, do not fear: nobody does. Those who say they understand the options market are either lying or deluding themselves. The latter will lose a great deal of money in a very short time. So will the former, actually.

COMMODITIES - In the old days, these were restricted to things people might want - like cocoa, coffee or tin. But this has changed. How would you like to take delivery of 10,000 pork bellies, or 5,000 gallons of frozen fox urine?

CHARACTERS

The City is a jungle, populated by an array of animals. Each business area has its own distinct role and attracts its own distinct type of bastard. Not everyone wants the same thing. Not everyone uses the same methods. Not everyone has the same ethics (or lack of them). Before you stab that back, you must know what type of back it is, and where the armour is weakest:

CORPORATE FINANCIERS

The deal-makers. The men behind the flotations, the hostile bids, the leveraged buy-outs. In short, the aristocracy of the City.

Education - Any major public school will do, as long as it has unheated dormitories, fagging and bad food. This will be followed by either Oxford or Cambridge (no other university will do, although some of the particularly well-connected avoid higher education altogether)

Family - Top corporate financiers find a wife a necessary irritant who may be telephoned at 8pm and told that her husband is on a flight to New York or Milan, or telephoned on Friday night and told he has gone ski-ing with clients, but who has to be produced occasionally in order to dispel rumours of homosexuality (which actually are true). The best corporate financiers have not seen their wives for five years. Children *are* needed, otherwise nepotism would have to devolve to nephews and nieces

Home - A house in the country for weekends, and a flat in the Barbican during the week

Clothes - Hand-tailored pin-stripe suits, hand-made pin-stripe shirts, Hermes ties, Church's half-brogues, ladies' underwear

Car - Chauffeur-driven Daimler, with two mobile telephones and a Reuter's screen

Clubs - White's, City Club, Pinstripe Club (where scantily dressed but mature women apply correction)

Drinking - Tomato juice with Worcester Sauce (virgin Mary) before lunch, Highland Spring water with lunch; a glass of Chateau Lafitte Rothschild 1971 with dinner, and a 60-years old Armagnac after

Recreations - Ski-ing (with clients), shooting (with clients), opera (with clients), flagellation (as a client)

Politics - Makes donations to the Conservative Party, but is too busy to vote

Favourite phrases - 'I think it would be best for all concerned if . . . ', 'Of course he will agree, he was my fag at school . . . ', 'I'm afraid that course of action would not be in the best interests of my client. *However* . . . ', 'My fee is . . . '

Ambition - Non-executive chairmanship of a large public limited company by the age of 40

STOCKBROKING ANALYSTS

The back-room boys. However, in recent years - due to appearances on television and articles in the press - they have deluded themselves into thinking people listen to them. This is a dangerous misconception.

Education - Grammar school (preferably northern), redbrick university (or minor Oxbridge college) where they read something useful like accountancy or chemistry

Family - Wife who was a nurse (or some similar worthy occupation) and is willing to get up at 4am so that her husband can be in the office by 5.30am. No children (too tired to procreate)

Home - Semi-detached in Walton-on-Thames

Clothes - Ill-fitting suit from M&S or Next, greying white M&S shirt, grey socks, scuffed Hush Puppies with plastic soles

Car - Anything Japanese, as long as it does more than 40 miles to the gallon

Clubs - Nathaniel Fatbastard's gym and / or squash club which is 2 minutes from the office, Walton-on-Thames Rotary Club

Drinking - Lots of coffee in the morning, occasional warm half-pint of beer in the pub after work

Recreations - Rugger, cricket, staying in the office at weekends to complete in-depth reports, finding excuses for why the last recommendation was wrong

Politics - Votes Liberal, but is too scared to admit it

Favourite phrases - 'Hold' (meaning Sell), 'Strong hold' (Hold), 'Buy' (Hold, but they are corporate clients), 'Strong buy' (I really mean it), 'Sell' (I've been offered another job)

Ambition - To be a corporate financier

MARKET MAKERS

The traders - the people who make the market work.

Education - Gants Hill Comprehensive, Borstal

Family - Girlfriend called Chantelle (who is a beautician and wears mini-skirts with no tights in midwinter, and stiletto shoes so high she suffers from altitude sickness), a pit-bull terrier called Killer

Home - Mock-Tudor mansion in Chigwell

Clothes - Italian suits from Woodhouse, Italian shirts from Woodhouse, loud ties, jogging bottoms

Car - White Ford Sierra XR4i Cosworth 4x4 turbo, with go-faster stripes and Vodafone

Clubs - Swankies (Romford), West Ham United supporters' club - the Intercity firm

Drinking - Champagne (swigged from the bottle) at lunchtime, 14 pints of lager in the evening

Recreations - Playing football, watching football, doing the football pools, dog-racing

Politics - National Front and Norman Tebbit

Favourite phrases - 'It's f***in' *buy*, innit?', 'It's a f***in' *sell*, innit?', 'Do wot?', 'My old ma could sell that, an' she's 75', 'I'm up to me f***in' neck in these bleedin' shares', 'Shit or get off the potty'

Ambition - To own a football club, or - failing that - a greyhound

EUROBOND TRADERS

A breed apart - specialists who play with their own market.

Education - US high school, Ivy League university, MIT, Harvard Business School, Insead [*in-se'ad*] (Fontainebleau)

Family - No wife, no children, telephones mother in Chicago on public holidays

Home - High-tech flat in Belgravia (smaller than his car), sleeps in the office

Clothes - Brookes Brothers suits with no shoulders, button-down shirts, Bass Weejun loafers, boxer shorts

Car - Porsche

Clubs - No time for them

Drinking - Does not drink, does not smoke, does not have sex, spends most of his six-figure salary on cocaine

Recreations - Telephoning analysts at 3am to ask about the yield on Japanese equity warrants and saying 'Did I wake you?'

Politics - 'Well, I naturally incline toward the Democratic party, but there is a lot to say for the policies of George Bush and the current administration'

Favourite phrases - 'The issue is going well' (We've sold about a fifth and are looking at a $5m loss), 'Market conditions are favourable' (My salary review is coming up), 'There is good institutional support' (I managed to sell some to a German pension fund), 'I'm afraid that is outside my remit' (That's your problem)

Ambition - To be transferred out of the London office before his mistakes catch up with him.

FUND MANAGERS

The buck stops here. These guys own everything, and are based in Edinburgh

Education - Fettes or some other miserable Scottish boarding school, St Andrew's University

Family - Wife who is a leading member of the Church of Scotland, at least seven children

Home - Poorly-heated detatched house (with grounds) in Morningside, Edinburgh

Clothes - Pin-stripes during the week, tweeds at weekends, sensible shoes

Car - Anything, as long as it is British, economical and comes in an estate version

Clubs - East Lothian Chamber of Commerce, local masonic lodge

Drinking - One whisky (with water) at Christmas

Recreations - Shooting and fishing, writing letters to the council about the state of roads, refuse collection, or cleanliness of roadsweepers

Politics - Has no time for such frivolity

Favourite phrases - 'No, I'll not be coming to London, you can visit me here', 'It's too expensive', 'They'll have to up the dividend', 'Aye, they look good value; I'll have 50'

Ambition - To retire to a croft in the Highlands

WOMEN IN THE CITY

There was a time when the only women in the City were secretaries who had three functions in life - making coffee, staying late to type up documents, and sleeping with their bosses. These women came in on the train from Barking, wore enough make-up to disguise Ronald Biggs, and had the ability to sound bored 25 hours a day. Although you still see them around, they are being supplanted by a whole new flock of breeds:

THE P.A.

THE PERSONAL ASSISTANT

A much-feared and much-respected animal. The PA is even more formidable than Margaret Thatcher in her 'You must understand, Sir Robin, . . . ' mode. If the Kuwaitis had had a line of PA's on their border, Saddam Hussein would never have invaded.

Age - Indeterminable.

Could be anything from 25 to 55. They all look the same

Dress - Smart Next suit with a dangerous brooch. Highlighted hair set in a vicious flick-back which looks as though it was constructed by Taylor Woodrow. Subtle but effective make-up

Home - Semi-detached in an upmarket suburb like Edgware

Family - Husband who earns less than she does, is good at DIY, and is scared to open his mouth. Two swotty children

Drinking - Mineral water at her desk (to wash down her M&S sandwiches), occasional gin and tonic

Accent - Supercilious pseudo-Sloane (wholly unnatural - product of years of elocution lessons)

Favourite phrases - 'He is in a meeting/at lunch/away on business', 'Would you give me your name, what company you're from, and a number where we can contact you', 'I'm sorry, he's very busy and cannot be disturbed', 'I'll decide whether he is free or not'

Ambition - To completely block any flow of information to her boss

THE GLAMOUR SLOANE

Started appearing in the early 1980s - first in public relations, then as junior stockbroking analysts and in the lower echelons of merchant banks. Who are these women, and where do they come from? Surely Roedean never had *that* many pupils?

Age - 22 to 35

Dress - Expensive designer suits (with short skirts to show off long, glorious legs which are perpetually crossed), tiny Chanel bags (with the strap worn sideways across the body, bisecting

THE GLAMOUR SLOANE

rather small breasts), long, swept-back blonde or black hair (often worn in a pony tail), minimal make-up (except for dark red lipstick)

Home - Flat in Fulham shared with two other girls - one working in a gallery, the other in advertising

Family - Father used to be in the City, brother is in the City, mother drinks

Drinking - bloody Mary, G & T, holds her liquor depressingly well. Eats rarely - and then only salad

Accent - Haughty, plummy, laughs like a horse

Favourite phrases - 'Gstaad was a nightmare', 'Of course he wanted to go to bed with me', 'Oh, I found it in a little shop in Milan', 'Darling, darling, darling', 'My horse is my only passion apart from you'

Ambition - To get a better job than her brother, then give it up to live in the country and ride horses

THE FRUMP

Appears at 6am and leaves at 10pm - beavers away in between. Everyone says they are the backbone of the merchant bank, but always passes over them for promotion.

Age - Late 30's, early 40's

Dress - Tweedy things that don't go with each other, white tights, sensible shoes, hair cut by Dewhurst the butcher, looks permanently disorganised

Home - Flat in Bayswater, or somewhere south of the river near a tube station

Family - Divorced, no children

THE FRUMP

Drinking - Black coffee with chocolate biscuits

Accent - Upper class and high-pitched

Favourite phrases - 'Yes, it will be done immediately', 'I'll be in on Sunday', 'If I could just remind you of ...'

Ambition - Dreams of being a top corporate financier, but will never make it because she lacks political nous

WHAT NOT TO DO

If the 1980s was a decade of daring - when fortunes were made or lost, when the the deal was done at any cost - then the 1990's is a decade of caution. The Stock Market crash, the Guinness trial, and the public vilification of Michael Milliken (the junk bond king) have forced upon the City a code of ethics unheard of in the past. Nobody believes 'My word is my bond' any longer. 'My word' has become a 100-page document, signed and counter-signed and binding until challenged in court. The cardinal rule is 'Do not agree to anything unless a lawyer is present'. And remember, this conversation is being taped.

Backstabbing - like everything else in the City - is coded and regulated. There are many 'do's' and 'don'ts' - though the most important 'don't' is still the Eleventh Commandment: 'Thou Shalt Not Be Found Out'. The true Backstabber will not necessarily avoid any activities because they are illegal or unethical, but will find ways of turning what was previously beyond the pale into an accepted part of everyday behaviour.

INSIDER DEALING - 'You should not trade on the basis of information that is not available to everyone else.' What nonsense! What is the point of trading on the basis of ignorance? That is a sure-fire way of losing money. Nowadays you still trade on the basis that you know something the other person does not know, but only if he does not know that you know what you know, and that there is no way that he can find out you know what you know, especially if you ought not to know what you know and he knows that.

BEAR RAIDS - A recent craze. This is when you spread false rumours of bad news to push down a share price so that you can pick up the shares more cheaply. There is now a law saying you cannot spread false rumours; if it was applied, most stockbroking analysts would be in prison. But to be on the safe side, get someone else to spread your false rumours for you - preferably a journalist.

ILLEGAL SHARE SUPPORT OPERATIONS - This was what the Guinness boys were caught doing: paying people to buy shares in their company. After a few of them were jailed, the City became worried that its brightest minds would wind up in Ford Open Prison (although the idea of forming a Ford Open Investment Trust is an attractive one). So in an attempt to stamp out illegal share supporting, the City decided that the law should be changed to make share support schemes legal.

JUNK BONDS - High-yielding bonds issued by companies which are virtually worthless. Everybody now realises that these were poor investments: if a company cannot pay its debts, it sure as hell cannot pay its junk bonds. But not wishing to junk (sorry!) a good idea, the City has now come up with 'mezzanine debt'. These are high-yielding bonds issued by companies which are virtually worthless.

MULTIPLE SHARE APPLICATIONS - Attempts by people to gain more than their fair share of the massive profits that result from privatisations, by putting in more than one application for shares. To combat this illegal activity, the Government decided to sanction multiple privatisations, so you can now apply for lots of different shares in the 7 water and sewerage businesses of England and Wales, or the 12 electricity companies. What next? The 13 regions of British Rail, the 47 area health authorities, and the 606 motorways?

CITY INSTITUTIONS AND REGULATORS

The best Backstabbers have an intimate knowledge not only of rules and regulations, but also who administers them. Manipulating the regulator is an art form perfected by the few, who cunningly persuade the authorities to administer the incision on their behalf. Here is a guide to the important regulators:

THE PANEL ON TAKE-OVERS AND MERGERS - A learned body comprised of real-life merchant bankers and lawyers. It hands down rulings of such unerring complexity that its executive council often cannot understand them. It has no formal powers, but in the public school atmosphere of the City a negative ruling is the equivalent of being made to stand in the corner in the dunce's cap, and everybody obeys. Arch Backstabbers go to great lengths to get the Panel on their side.

THE BANK OF ENGLAND - Much is made of the power of the Governor of the Bank of England's eyebrows. He has only to raise them for chairmen of merchant banks to hand in their resignations, or for companies to accept deals that are plainly not in their interests. What would happen if the Governor had a nervous tic?

THE DEPARTMENT OF TRADE AND INDUSTRY - Known as the Department of Timidity and Indolence, it is ultimately in charge of everything. Occasionally it appoints inspectors to investigate scandals, but the investigations take so long that by the time they complete their report everyone has forgotten what the scandal was - even if the report is published.

THE SERIOUS FRAUD OFFICE - Set up to investigate serious frauds - but apparently *not* to gain convictions, judging by its success rate. If investigated, the arch Backstabber should give an interview to a Sunday newspaper from his Paraguayan retreat saying that he is willing to co-operate fully with the SFO, but never actually talk to its officers.

THE STOCK EXCHANGE - A Kafka-esque body which has taken to City regulation like a leech to a nudist colony. Its insider dealing group investigates everything. If investigated, Backstabber should point the finger at somebody else (the Exchange is sure to be investigating them too). The Exchange's inefficiency is legendary, so if you are investigated, do not panic. They will eventually lose your file.

THE EUROPEAN COMMISSION - Has sweeping powers to investigate just about anything. Nobody understands how wide these powers are, so Backstabber only has to throw in a casual remark like 'Of course this could fall under Article 77 of the Treaty of Rome' to cause widespread panic and get whatever he wants.

THE OFFICE OF FAIR TRADING AND THE MONOPOLIES & MERGERS COMMISSION - Bodies set up to investigate anti-competitive trading practices, which of course proliferate - especially in the City. Before tangling with either of these bodies, Backstabber must check that the company he is working for makes large contributions to the Tory Party. If it does, he can relax: a Government minister will always save the day.

STRATEGIES FOR BACKSTABBING

Now that you know who does what to whom in which market, you are ready for the final lesson: backstabbing strategies. All the methods described in the section are mere outlines. Backstabber is as much of an artist as a jazz musician: everyone knows the tunes, but *he* will be able to improvise *ad infinitum*.

DAMNING WITH FAINT PRAISE - It is not *comme il faut* to attack colleagues openly in the City, so a code has evolved by which the knife can be applied in the guise of a bouquet. For example:

'A loyal and trusted colleague' (He was too stupid to find a job anywhere else)

'We had a close working relationship' (Personally, I hated him)

'He is a close personal friend' (Otherwise he would have been sacked years ago)

'He is resigning to pursue other interests' (We sacked him)

'He is resigning for personal reasons' (He had his hand in the till)

'I am helping him with his punishing workload' (He has made a load of cock-ups and I am trying to sort them out)

'I would like to thank him for his hard endeavours' (Everything he touched was a disaster)

'I have the utmost faith in his abilities' (We can't find anyone willing to replace him)

THE STOCK EXCHANGE STATEMENT - One of the jewels in the Backstabber's crown. In the sea of lies and deceit in the City there is one rock of truth - the Company News Service run by The Stock Exchange. Everybody trusts it, and once something is announced on it, the City will believe what it reads. This is when Backstabber strikes. He puts his hand on his heart and tells the Exchange the supreme lie, which is published verbatim. This strategy would never work with the press (who might ask difficult questions) or stockbrokers (who could easily decide that the lie was a lie if not presented as the truth on their dealing screens).

THE CLARIFICATION STATEMENT - An even more subtle and refined version of the above. Backstabber identifies a hostile press article, an analysts report or even a rumour, and puts out a Stock Exchange Statement clarifying the situation. A clarification is rarely a denial, but a cleverly-worded version of the truth that discredits a correct story; or - failing that - which muddies the water sufficiently so that nobody knows what to believe.

THE PRESS - Manipulation of the press is a skill Backstabber must acquire, as it will be one of the best weapons in his armoury. There are several ways to choose from:

The Friday night drop - a practice that has become part of tradition. (Age-old Backstabbers are amazed it still works, but it does.) Backstabber - or preferably his grovelling public relations man - telephones a Sunday newspaper journalist on Friday night with a piece of information. The journalist is told to call Backstabber the next day, but finds the number unobtainable or permanently engaged, and that there is no-one else to talk to. Thus he is forced to either ignore a potentially good story, or run it unchecked. Backstabber will always resist the temptation to pass on complete fiction, for he knows that in order to keep the fish hooked in the future his information must contain some small element of truth (which he hopes will not find its way into the final newspaper article).

The 7.30pm Telephone Call - a shorter, more immediate - if less subtle - version of the above, but useful for dealing with daily newspapers. If a reporter is trying to contact you, do not ring back until 7.30pm, which - with luck - will be the writer's deadline. Any information imparted will go straight into the article as there will be no time to get it verified. An intimate knowledge of journalists' deadlines is part of the Backstabber's art.

The Off-the-record Comment - without a doubt the best way to manipulate information. This is when you confide a piece of intelligence in a journalist or analyst and they promise never to say it came from you. (It must be distinguished from a 'non-attributable comment', which the journalist is free to repeat to a member of the Fraud Squad, should he so wish. Or 'deep background', which can be interpreted as meaning just about anything.) The purpose of the off-the-record comment is:

- to make the recipient feel he will look extremely clever when it is repeated in print
- to deceive him into believing he is in your sole confidence (whereas in fact you have told half the City)
- to plant the most outrageous lies without anyone realising it was you (see 'Bear Raids' above).

The Lawyer's Telephone Call - if a journalist seems reluctant to print your fake story, get your lawyer to call and threaten all sorts of things should the story appear - such as writs, injunctions, no bottles of whisky at Christmas, etc. Any journalist worth his salt will think there *must* be a scandal afoot and print the story immediately.

CLIENT CONFIDENTIALITY - The City Backstabber knows that it is unethical to release confidential information about clients. Sticking to this rule would make it almost impossible to work in the City, so the Backstabber's credo is 'If it does you any good, it is not confidential; and if it could be harmful, it *is* confidential'. Stockbrokers' reports are a good example: some brokers maintain they cannot make share recommendations for companies who are their clients (this is usually only when the recommendation would be 'Sell').

MERGERS AND ACQUISITIONS - Another art of a City Backstabber is to be able to persuade a client to buy a company, then sell it again a couple of years later, thus generating large fees. If a company is doing well in one area, Backstabber should persuade them to diversify, saying they need a second / third / fourth leg. If the acquisition goes well, Backstabber can later persuade them into a demerger to maximise shareholder value. If it goes badly, there is the opportunity to dispose of a 'non-core' business. And if it goes really badly, Backstabber should persuade the management to stand down (he can subsequently gain large fees and much kudos by finding a new management for the group).

RESIGNING ON A POINT OF PRINCIPLE - Everybody knows that if you work in the City you have no principles. Therefore resigning on the point of one is a tricky manoeuvre that should only be used once. However, the *threat* can often be used - particularly when a client or employer is failing to do what you want. Backstabber knows they know he has acted unethically on many occasions with their blessing, but for him to pull one of these skeletons out of the closet would spell disaster, so they will not call his bluff. Backstabber never concedes defeat unless a scandal has grown so large it can only be contained by putting up a smoke-screen with his timely resignation. The scandal can then be hushed up and he is free to go and work for another City firm.

ACCOUNTANTS - The City Backstabber knows that accountancy is an art, not a science. The manipulation of standard accounting practice to make black appear white is a much sought-after skill. The best accountant is one whose answer to the question 'What does two and two make?', is 'What number did you have in mind?' The stewards of company's accountants are called 'auditors'. These are useful to dupe, cajole and - if things go wrong - blame. And if all else fails, you can sue them.

. . . . and that was the point when the Hon Perry stopped. He leaned over and grasped me by the Jasper Conrans. 'And do you know what gets right up my nose?' he growled, ' After 25 years of shafting, scraping and knifing to get to the top of the pile, I don't like the view. The City sold out to those bastards in Osaka and Munchengladbach and now they've got the Square Mile by the balls. We've stabbed ourselves in the back, old boy.'

With that, he stood up and shook my hand. Then the Hon Peregrine Crookes-Arntwe - City legend and Backstabber *par excellence* - set off back to the office, pausing on his way to pay a discreet call on his harem of young boys.

TELEVISION

by Francesca Bid

So *you* think you want to work in television. Well, forget it, unless you have a skin thicker than a rhinoceros. To succeed in television in the 1990's requires a ruthlessness and resilience that makes the Spanish Inquisition look like the Salvation Army.

In days gone by, the BBC alone ruled the (air)waves, and the world of television was full of well-intentioned programme-makers content to inform and entertain. Today, with the advent of commercial stations, television has become a battleground in the war of the ratings.

But if you are coming to television because you like the idea of educating the masses, coupled with the supposed glamour of a Hollywood lifestyle, think again. The motto of today's television world is 'Never mind the quality, feel the width'. The old priorities of content and style have given way to vying over viewing figures and prime time slots.

One thing remains the same however: the hunger for new programme ideas. As the number of stations bidding for your evening's viewing has increased over the last three decades, so too has the need for innovative concepts to hold the attention of a fickle public. New ideas are like gold dust, and as the viewing audience becomes more sophisticated, the continual demand for something original to seduce them to your channel challenges your very survival.

READY STEADY...

Are you armed with relentless ambition? Good. Without it, you will find it impossible to indulge in the skullduggery required to get you where you want to be - i.e. the last and - paradoxically - longest credit lingering on screen as the music fades. If you play your cards right, you may even reach the bottom within ten years!

Before you start, here is some useful jargon:

Blag - To wangle a coveted book, record or similar item from the promoter by pretending you intend to do a programme on the author or artist
Development money - Money given by commissioning editors to independent producers to research their proposals for programmes
Dumping - Passing the buck
Networking - Hanging out with television bigwigs for gossip or promotion purposes
Winging it - Making it up as you go along

...GO!

There are regular openings in television, despite the thousands of people who apply for every job advertised. The disenchanted say this is largely due to its similarity to McDonald's both in rate of turnover and - in the case of satellite television - quality control. Most programmes are made over a 6 to 12 month period, and the staff (or 'Crew') are brought in from within the industry. Contracts are issued to those considered best at the job (or who happen to be free at the time), so there is always an opportunity for the professional Backstabber to scupper his opponents and seize the moment.

Your career plan depends on your 'previous'. All the usual criteria - such as education, accent and contacts - will apply here, so it is advisable to decide as soon as possible which labels fit, and target the appropriate station:

BBC1 - They pretend not to care where you come from, but - as with the Tory Cabinet - Oxbridge credentials find most favour. All posts are gained by working up from the bottom.

BBC2 - Left-wing views, beards and sandals are a must if you work in the *Open University* department, but otherwise this is the sorting-house of ivy-league universities and classless, frighteningly bright, mavericks. These may be identified by their serious looks and lack of dress sense.

ITV/SKY - Fast becoming indistinguishable from each other, these two tabloid channels attract ex-journalists with a penchant for anal humour and pneumatic blondes. No previous experience necessary.

CHANNEL 4 - Definitely *Guardian* and *Independent* readers only, who have transferred from other professions, bringing a bulging contacts file with them. If you are a suburban, one-legged 'minority' gay, and have a friend who can lend the crew a camera, so much the better.

Having selected your station, you must arm yourself with information. This means resigning yourself to a week's concentrated television-watching, notebook in hand to list important names gleaned from the credit rolls. Then get hold of a copy of *Broadcast* and see which shows get the highest ratings. Pin-point those lowest on the list and compose a paragraph on 'How I think the show could be improved'. When you are interviewed, this will be the first question the producer will ask you. Praise *Newsnight,* but say you cannot help loving Jeremy Beadle. This will give the impression that you are a person of substance who - if pressed - would not mind being transferred to a game show in difficult times. Last - but by no means least - put forward a couple of programme ideas of your own. If they are good, the producer will snap you up with the intention of 'borrowing' future concepts from you to further his own career. If they are bad, you will be taken on in the belief that you are unlikely ever to challenge his job.

RUNNING UP

Where should you begin your career? In television, it is important to be seen never to have made a mistake (mistakes can be very expensive indeed - *vide* BSB), so aim low at a job you can handle with your eyes shut - but not so low that you cannot pass the buck one rung lower when you hit trouble. If you lack a good academic background or other career 'previous', then the post of 'runner' is a good starting point. Being a runner or camera assistant is not a glamorous job - it is the television equivalent of a film 'gofer' - you 'run' errands. Errands include making coffee and shifting furniture, as well as running to the 'drug' store for the senior members of the crew. With luck, you will be allowed to go out 'on a shoot', drive the company van, or even carry the lights to the location. Fortunately for the far-sighted Backstabber, the post is usually taken by beautiful young men who are drawn to the glamour of television. They spend a great deal of time smoking Marlboro cigarettes, eyeing up the researchers and trying to look busy or cool. They are flirtatious, lazy and think being cheeky is clever - they will never succeed.

Backstabbers - *carpe diem*! These hapless opponents are green. *You* will give the bosses just what they want - reliability and enthusiasm. On them, your willingness to perform any required task, however menial, will have precisely the right effect. Your awe-inspiring enthusiasm and admiring obsequiousness will massage their egos in just the right spot.

Whether your aspirations lie in the technical or the creative top echelons, you must use your time as a runner to learn the trade and the essential tele-jargon. Volunteer for everything, whether it be hanging around an 'edit suite' to fetch bacon sandwiches for the director or keeping guard while the van is parked on double yellow lines in the rush hour. This is all 'spying time': learn who is doing what, where and to whom. A fount of informed gossip and slander will be one of your most useful assets later on - start early and watch how the professionals do it.

Dress - Men: ripped Levi's, corduroy shirts and baseball caps, clean shaven. Try to exude the raw sexual energy and hidden

emotional depths of James Dean (this will endear you to female bosses, while not threatening senior males with power-dressing). Women: spray-on jeans and lycra tops. Hair - à la Kylie (different every day) or the short, gamine look. A good body will help get you a place as someone's assistant and - if packaged properly - a bit-part on camera.
Time - About a year to eighteen months. Move up any faster and other runners will start rumours about you granting sexual favours to the producer.
Age - You can never be too young, but over 25's look ridiculous in lycra (ditto baseball caps)

BENDING AN EAR

The next step up is the post of researcher. Find a soon-to-be-vacant post and slip your application - containing an irresistibly reasonable salary request - onto the boss's desk the day before the ad. goes into the *Guardian*.

Making the leap from runner to researcher requires more work. Become an expert on something - it is not important what (gardening and politics are already bespoken) - then stay behind after office hours and 'borrow' all the useful numbers you can find from the contacts books of other researchers. Take every opportunity to drop comments like 'I've got a friend in . . . ' or 'Madonna's brother is a mate of mine . . . ' - you can be very economical with the truth! The true Backstabber researcher will possess the ability to insinuate his way through any closed door.

You will have to do *a great deal* of work - mostly on the telephone - finding whacky, exotic but cheap locations, and cajoling celebrities or members of the public to appear or give advice for free, so make sure you develop the 'Of course, if *I* were holding the purse-strings . . . ' approach. Contrive to sound sympathetic but hassled - it always works. When under pressure, be evasive: 'I've got a call on the other line . . . '. If all else fails, disconnect the lead - much the easiest way of avoiding calls from pushy agents or weird religious eccentrics.

The true Backstabber will use idle moments to 'lig' or 'blag' promotional books and records for the directors and producers in

return for an afternoon off or - if you have your eye on presenting - for permission to 'do the interview' yourself. Such toadying may also entitle you to make humble suggestions in the edit suite about the look of the final cut. But don't overdo it - these guys were once Backstabber researchers themselves and can smell ambition a mile off.
Dress - Men: according to the nature of the programme. If it is a 'doco' (documentary), go for shabby suits and brogues; if it is 'LE' (light entertainment), dress your bottom half like a runner and your top half like Next. Women: according to the nature of your boss. If he is a man, the micro black miniskirt and tailored jacket is *de rigueur*; if she is a woman, dress like her - but cheaper (emulation will get you everywhere).
Time - I have never known a researcher get away with less than 2 years on the circuit. Be patient.
Age - If you are still there at 30, you have probably missed the boat - or you are too good at your job!

PRESENTING THE CASE

Everyone wants to be a presenter - everybody, that is, who does not actually work in television. To the outsider it suggests glamour, free trips, hobnobbing with celebrities and an unlimited clothes allowance. To the insider it means taking more orders than an overworked waiter and doing more hours than a junior doctor on call. Admittedly pay is high, but it has to be. Why else would anyone submit to being called out at 3am to cover a story down a coal mine, or being forced by the director to test-ride a unicycle? And in the studio with your guest, it is *your* job to fill the gap that so often yawns between question and answer. Some presenters thrive on waffle and have perfected the art of interrogation: these are the real pros and are treated accordingly. Any rumours you hear about David Frost getting away with outrageous prima donna tantrums, or Cilla Black getting £30,000-plus per episode for *Blind Date*, are true.

Presenting is a very long shot indeed, even for the arch Backstabber. In 'yoof' programming (the only area that has not been commandeered by Gloria Hunniford, Jeremy Beadle and

Chris Tarrant), there has been, in recent years, an increasing trend towards the 'unusual' - so if you look or sound normal, your chances of seeing yourself on screen are minimal. Count the number of 'ethnic' women and wide-boy cheeky chappies fronting shows, and you will see what I mean.

However, if you *are* lucky enough to pass your screen test, a few words of advice: be a sport, and be super-humble. Presenting is the only job in television where it is important to be nice. Even if you are hopeless at the job, you can be so nice that everyone is too fond of you to say so - and voilà! - the second series is born. But a word of caution: always keep your options open, for the course of true stardom never runs smooth. If ratings are low, producers always blame it on the presenter, and many a higher flier than you has come an abrupt cropper.

Dress - No rules here for either sex, but study the appalling outfits in the House of Commons and wear the opposite.
Time - As long as you stay in fashion
Age - Irrelevant for men. Women are over the hill when soft lighting can no longer cheat the wrinkles, or when they outgrow a size 10.

TICKET TO RIDE

If office politics are your idea of a drag, you belong out on the road with the film crew. These technical wizards do not really belong in *The Backstabber's Guide*, since there is no way you can fake their specialist know-how. However, Backstabber will find it useful to be able to identify them, and their duties, when faking his own filming experience:

LIGHTING CAMERAMAN - He is usually tall, wears an expensive leather jacket, and has a beer gut to match his height - an essential physical attribute needed to counterbalance the considerable weight of the camera and the ludicrous positions the director asks him to adopt. In theory, his principal function is to decide what lights to use, but in practice it is to save the shoot from the director's misconceived ideas of what constitutes an

THE CREW WHO SPEND THE BUDGET ....

interesting shot. That is why producers are prepared to pay an experienced cameraman up to £300 a day.

SOUND ENGINEER - He is the guy in the anorak, holding what looks like a fat, fur-covered sausage on a stick. Otherwise recognisable by a complete lack of humour or conversation, and with an extra supply of sandwiches packed by his loving mother.

.... THE NIGHTWATCHMAN WHO GUARDS IT

CAMERA ASSISTANT - Another name for the runner brought along to drive the van and unload the equipment. His ego is

inflated by the prospect of one day becoming a fully-fledged cameraman, and he is easily identified by his ostentatious use of obscure lighting terms and his infuriatingly irrelevant advice to the director. He starts every sentence with a sharp intake of breath and 'I don't think you should do that, mate'.

GOOD HOUSEKEEPING

While the crew relax in the pub after their 13-hour day, celebrating the fact that they are the only people in independent television to be paid overtime, the production manager sits in the office behind a mountain of lever arch files, invoices and assorted forms - a tortured, gibbering wreck clinging desperately to the petty cash box. He is responsible for controlling the budget.

A thankless task by any definition, production management is not for those who fear mounds of paperwork or sums. However, if you are one of those who enjoy the challenge of squeezing blood out of a financial stone, it will be your responsibility to budget the entire operation, from finding the cheapest film crew to dealing with contributors claiming back taxi fares.

Astonishingly, this job is often filled by decent, friendly production secretaries and assistants who found themselves unexpectedly promoted when the last decent, friendly production manager was taken away by men in white coats. Too humble to recognise that they have been given an impossible task, they lapse into PMT (Production Manager Trauma), identified by permanent irritability, paranoia and - in the worst cases - making a nest of all the invoices and falling hopelessly in love with their main persecutor - the married and unobtainable series editor.

But as a Backstabber - with your natural amorality, duplicity and criminal mind - *you* will not fail to capitalise on this magnificent opportunity. Ideally, like the best Machiavellian production managers, you should have a degree in economics and a spell as a stock market trader under your belt. Thus equipped with creative accounting skills, juggling - rather than stretching - money will be your forte. Here - by dint of studying your employer's accounting books (you may blackmail them shamelessly if later threatened with exposure) - you will discover how to convert funds for a Channel 4 documentary on old age into a new Mercedes, and utilise your time honing your special art of redirecting the contents of the petty cash box into, say, your own 'location research' holiday in Antibes.

Dress - Smart but casual. Anything too flashy and your superiors will start checking the costume budget. Those working on nature or outside location shows should go for the 'ready for action' look - Barbour or Puffa jacket and a cellnet telephone.

Age - Young enough to flirt over the telephone with aggressive debt collectors, but old enough to play the stern parent if things get ugly.

THE EMPEROR'S NEW CLOTHES

Your next rung up the ladder is director. You are the one with your feet on the desk, always on the telephone picking up offers of work waiting on your home answerphone. What bugs the production manager is not your demands for exotic lenses, ludicrous expenses invoices or even your abuse of office facilities; it is the fact you are so damned laid back when all around is frenzied chaos.

As a director you will be expected to turn limp, hazy ideas into visionary feasts, while creating an exciting and cogent line of thought out of a wooden script or badly-typed notes from a resentful researcher. On the shoot you will have to combat torrential rain, recalcitrant camera crews, battery failures, spoilt presenters and actors, unyielding interviewees (both two- and four-legged), and live audiences who laugh in the wrong places - and still come back with stunning close-ups and long-shots, without going into overtime.

So how do you manage to look so calm, so laconic, so playful? The backstabbing director's art is his ability to create an aura of serenity, an air of mystique - you must never get ruffled and never give *anything* away. You are concerned with making everything you do look good, and you realise that beauty - or rather talent - is firmly in the eye of the beholder. You must look so confident that those around you, riddled with their own self-doubt, assume you are so professional that you can do your job with your eyes shut;

and rather than betray their own inadequacies, they will all bend over backwards to try and match *your* standards. Then abracadabra! The award-winning programme is made, you have retained your sanity, *and* gained that much-coveted last credit at the end of the show - all your skulduggery has paid off!

But be prepared for one minor indignity - slander. Television people eat gossip for breakfast, and your cool air of mystery may rancour. Do not be offended if you hear that you are 'doing it' with Janet Street Porter, or that you are into rubberware - for the more ludicrous the rumour, the more revered you will become. In any case, such prurient smears can save you a fortune on business cards - no-one will forget your name, and that is a big plus in a freelance world.

As a coda, I must add that there are an ever-increasing number of female directors entering the field. Their methods are less mysterious but equally effective: favours are won from female co-workers by alleging menstrual cramps and sharing heartbreak stories, while the males are won over by adopting a pleading baby voice interspersed with Goldie Hawn giggles.

Dress - Men: notoriously appalling, without a clue about colour coding, style or fit; the idea is to confuse and mislead, but ends up looking like Man at C&A. Women: like *Playschool* presenters - all bright colours and Kickers, or walking advertisements for Levi's.
Age - Under 27 and you are too young to have had a mysterious past. Over 50 and you should have been invited to Hollywood by now.

IT'S A DOG'S LIFE

Every master has his dog, and that is what you rise to next - the 'associate producer'. This much-coveted title is every researcher's and production manager's dream - their entrée into the inner sanctum where all the 'ideas' people live. The post ought to give you licence to do all the *nice* things that producers do - call meetings, hire and fire with impunity, go for long lunches and command a huge salary. In reality all you will get is their dirty work on top of your old duties, time for a quick sandwich (if you are lucky), and the money you *should* have been getting as a researcher. For 'associate producer', read 'dogsbody'.

Nevertheless the post is very useful and should be treated as your final term at finishing school. In six months, associate producers can learn a great deal about getting a programme off the paper and onto the screen. You will be doing everything the producer does (bar enjoying the above-mentioned perks) and will have the opportunity to study him (or her - for many producers in television are women) closely. Observant Backstabbers may quickly smell a familiar calculating rat. They will note the 3-hour lunches at Groucho's, the telephone calls from 'friends' talking contracts and money in hushed voices, the casual enquiries about so-and-so's availability and agent's number, and - most telling of all - the frequency of your producer's late arrival dressed in his best suit.

Two and two make four: your producer is simply availing himself of the boss's facilities and *your* overtime to try and set up his own production company. Armed with this information, backstabbing associate producers have two options open to them: either they 'snitch' to the company boss, or they join the traitor as an on-site accomplice. Your best move is to leak the news to a notoriously indiscreet researcher; then quietly mention to the producer that when he has set up his company, you (as the replacement producer with your *own* hard-working associate producer!) will have plenty of time to do some unofficial freelance work for him - 'We could always meet up for lunch at Groucho's!'

Dress - Same as for researcher or production manager, but accentuate new status by addition of Butler & Wilson jewellery, or silk tie and Paul Smith jacket.

Age - Around 28 (or once you are mature enough to understand it is better to sell your soul than lose your mortgage). Still being there in your 30's is no indication of lack of talent, but simply a sign that your producer has so far failed to get his secret projects off the ground.

DEAR OLD AUNTIE

For those hopeful producers more interested in maintaining power and status than increasing their cash flow, the BBC is the natural choice. Like the Foreign Office or Civil Service, once you are in they will never get you out, and you can work your way up the ranks, acquiring more and more shouting power - and commensurate increments to your average (but reliable) salary - as you go.

At the Beeb, producers 'maintain' position. Unlike their independent counterparts, those working for Auntie cling to their titles like bull-terriers, as they are unlikely to rise any higher within the organisation. More importantly, 'producer' not only means overseeing the troops and budget, but also some hands-on directing and editing as well - an attractive job for those bent on total executive and artistic control.

It is therefore unsurprising to find that most BBC producers are either fiercely aggressive left-wing Oxbridge high fliers, or 40-something twinset-and-pearls headmistress types. Both are eager to prove themselves - the former to their right-wing parents, the latter to justify the twenty years it has taken them to work up from 'Used Stamp Sorter' on *Blue Peter*.

Even Backstabbers will need to start at the bottom, with a typing proficiency of 100 wpm and a working knowledge of coffee filter machines. Alternatively, take an associate producer's job in the independent sector and wait for a BBC programme's ratings to drop: that is when Auntie starts to panic and goes hunting for 'new blood'. 'Yoof' programming at the Beeb currently has a 'positive discrimination' policy; and lack of experience is a 'must' here (they claim it bestows a fresh new television style, but one suspects plain lack of cash).

Dress - BBC documentary producers favour radical Oxfam; the rest prefer M&S or Laura Ashley. 'Yoof' producers wear distressed leather jackets or 'crucial' casuals.
Age - Nothing under 30 (unless you work on 'DEF II', in which case you are past it)

THE OTHER SIDE OF THE COIN

But the astute Backstabber producer soon realises that the *real* money is earned by the executive producers who run the independent companies. Two or three good original ideas, some development money from the broadcasters and hey presto! - a company is born. Which is all very well, but what sticks in every in-house producer's throat is that while *he* is expected to come up with new and ever better ideas, the executive producers are creaming off the handsome production fees (the television equivalent of a retailer's mark-up).

So you join the club: you sneak out of the office to meet privately with commissioning Editors, huddle in corners at Groucho's with directors and production managers, spend guilty mornings with your accountant or commercial estate agent, and get your accomplices to start booking stars, venues and crew on the Q.T. When you have finally got it all together, you march into the boss's office and throw your resignation on the desk, inform him that you are off to be your own executive producer - that you are going to make some *honest* television, and - oh! by the way - you are taking half his team with you. You might make it, you might not - it is a very chancy business. If your programme tops the viewing charts, there will be another series. But if it comes at the bottom, you will be left with nothing but an empty in-tray and the dismal sight of your disillusioned staff crawling back to your old boss, taking their programme ideas and your stationery supplies with them.

STRIVING FOR THE TOP

You are almost there. You have learned the hard way that to be a successful television Backstabber requires a great deal of hard work and eyes in the back of your head. Throughout, your competitors will have set you up, abused your talents, stolen your best ideas *and* the best years of your life. Are riches and power sufficient reward for all the affronts and insults, the snubs and the exploitation? What you need to make the long hard slog worthwhile is *revenge*. Having made your reputation with at least one good show, now is the time to compile your hit list and apply for the post of commissioning editor (frequent vacancies arise from the high incidence of fatal cirrhosis of the liver among the incumbents). In whichever department you end up - be it as Head of Drama, Documentaries or even Religious Programming - you will be perfectly placed to carry out all the top-grade backstabbing you desire to retire avenged and in peace.

As a commissioning editor, *you* decide what programmes should be made with the department's budget, and in which restaurant to spend the expense account that often equals it. It is *you* who decides whether wildlife programmes with candid close-ups of bonking buffaloes should be broadcast at suppertime, whether *Blind Date* can stand three more series, or whether *Newsnight* should do another 'Who will win the next General Election' special. More importantly, you are also responsible for new commissions, i.e. giving money to independent production companies to develop and even execute new programme ideas. Are you beginning to get the picture?

You will be inundated with scripts for new plays, proposals for yet more documentaries on the sex life of the sperm whale, and outlines for innovative series on living authors. These will be followed by sycophantic telephone calls with offers of expensive lunches from their originators - including some names with whom by now you will be very familiar.

You may now exact revenge on your selected victims. Get your secretary to ring them back and tell them to spend some more time on their ideas. Suggest they take you out to lunch in a month's time to 'brainstorm' that series on living authors. Get them to develop the idea and persuade them to re-mortgage their house to finance a six-part series. String them along with vague promises. In two years' time they will be back with a completed series, a very anxious bank manager and a divorce. Let them down gently. You had doubts from the beginning: a series on 'living authors' had built-in obsolescence - four of the original six subjects are now 'ghost writers in the sky'!

THE ULTIMATE JOB

In television, it is the Station Controller's job to which you finally aspire. All need for backstabbing now comfortably behind you, the prime requisite will be to sit tight and display the diplomacy of a Wise Monkey - hear no evil, speak no evil, and - above all - see no evil . . . . and that includes watching television.

JOURNALISM

by Christian Wolmar

THE FIRST STAB

Journalism is *la crème de la crème* when it comes to the Backstabber's choice of professions. The very essence of success in Journalism is to learn to stitch people up - first the punters, then your rival newspapers, and finally your colleagues. The skills learned in shafting punters and rivals are easy for Backstabber to adapt and turn on colleagues. Indeed, journalists' love of plunging the dagger in between the shoulder blades was very nearly immortalised in the 1960's when *The Daily Mirror* asked the brewery who owned the pub on the ground floor of the new *Mirror* building whether it could be called 'The Stab', short for stab in the back. The brewery said no, but it made no difference: to this day, *Mirror* journalists call it 'The Stab' and conduct their dirty business there.

Journalism is replete with dirty business. There is a constant stream of deals being made between senior executives, concerning who will stay and who will go in the next purge of the old guard, and, as jobs in Fleet Street are never advertised, they also choose the bright young things who will replace them. These purges are a regular feature of all Fleet Street papers - particularly the tabloids - as circulations constantly fluctuate, and the journalists get blamed for the falls, while the Editor takes the credit for the rises.

SOME TERMS FOR STARTERS

Exclusive - a story no other newspaper in its right mind would print, or which has been published the day before (or even the year before) in a rival newspaper

Pack - a group of newshounds baying for a juicy story

Stake-out - time spent outside the home of a victim waiting to grill him

Contacts Book - what normal people call their address book

By-line - owning up to writing, or claiming to write, a story

Fleet Street - the collective name for national newspapers, even though none have their offices there now, and few ever did

Editor - the proprietor's sidekick

News Editor - the Editor's sidekick who runs the news pages, and who will not shrink from calling a reporter out at 7am to cover a foggy motorway crash and again at 11pm on the same day to cover a pub brawl

Chief Sub - person in control of the Sub-Editors and all those who sit on the 'back bench'

Sub-Editors - those who cut the stories to fit the page - either nip and tuck or slash and burn, depending on whether or not they like you - and who ensure that your story complies with the paper's editorial and political policies

Splash - the main front page story, likely to make waves

BOTTOM OF THE PILE

Journalism has no real career structure. There is only one Editor on a paper, a handful of executives, and 'the rest' of the journalistic staff. These last are the 'hacks' or 'grubbies'. There are two sorts: the Writers and the Subs (or Sub-Editors). Writers, general reporters and speclialists get all the glory, their name in the paper, the chance to travel the world, and the opportunity to compare the relative merits of all the Hilton Hotels en route.

Subs are the hidden cogs of the newspapers: they correct and proof the 'copy' (articles), write the headlines, fit the story into the page, and get shouted at by prima donna writers who resent every comma change. The Subs sit at computers all day, have incredibly unsocial hours (usually working from early afternoon to midnight), and are universally despised by the writers as failed reporters. But Subs have a host of ways of getting their revenge. Since they are the last people to see the copy and they write the headlines, they can ruin a story from a reporter they don't like. The simplest method is to omit the by-line. (At *The Independent*, during one of the periodic anti-smoking purges in the News Room, smokers who persisted in having a drag in the office had their by-lines removed from their stories. There was uproar.) The good backstabbing Sub can also deliberately fail to correct spelling mistakes, or even insert new ones.

The ultimate aim for Backstabber is to become Editor of a Fleet Street paper, although one could do worse than settle for a comfortable executive job with an expensive car and an unlimited expense allowance. There are two alternative routes to the top - by being a Sub or by staying a reporter. While the reporter may get the initial glory and his name in the paper, cunning Backstabber may choose the other route. This may involve years at a desk, stuck in front of a computer screen, but precisely *because* it is an office-based job, Backstabber can plot endlessly in office politics. But either way, the first thing to do is to get a job - and everyone starts as a reporter - and the second is to reach Fleet Street.

GETTING A FOOT ON THE LADDER

Traditionally, there were two ways up the journalist's career ladder. You could become an office boy (a bit tricky for women), running messages between departments or taking down copy for the journalists. Providing you took every opportunity to spread rumours, you were destined for success: rumours such as how so-and-so was no longer up to it, or how old Smith never came back from lunch before 4pm and always left on the dot of 5pm. Then when the Editor confirmed your information about old Smith, who do you think got Smith's job? You of course.

This route, alas, is now largely defunct. Computers have removed the necessity for paper, and with it the need for office boys. There may still be the odd job left in the canteen or the post room which might offer scope to meet a few journalists, but nothing that would ever appeal to Backstabber.

Getting a job on a provincial paper is the other possibility. There are two options - the weeklies and the dailies (which are usually published in the evening). Weeklies are the sleepiest of these institutions, often run by little more than an Editor in a sports jacket, his mature secretary, and a couple of young newshounds who write reams of turgid copy about the local parish council meetings and the opening of garden fêtes. Although this level of journalism is usually best avoided by all but the most desperate, it is useful as a starter - provided it is not for long. Once branded as a weekly journalist, abandon all hope. You will never catch Backstabber staying in one of these backwaters for more than a year or so.

Better by far to try the local daily paper. This will be a much more active operation - dozens of reporters and Subs, and any number of district staff who cover particular towns. There will even be a Features Editor and a Sports Editor. Here Backstabber will find three types of journalist: those on the way up, those on the way down, and those who have given up the ghost and settled for the provinces. These will be a host of earnest young men in over-sized suits, and a rather smaller number of ambitious women in under-sized skirts. The older reporters are probably those who have already tried and failed in Fleet Street - old soaks who have tasted a bit of the high life (possibly rather too much of it) - or those who have opted for a quiet life.

For a privileged few, there is Route One: Oxbridge, a holiday job at *The Spectator* or *The Economist*, preferably a relationship (sexual or blood) with a newspaper executive, and straight into Fleet Street on graduation day. This option, unfortunately, is only available to a few, and will not apply to most readers of this book.

THE SECOND STAB

Once you get a job on a provincial paper, you will learn that there are two entirely different worlds of journalism, each of which has an unhealthy contempt for the other - Fleet Street and the rest. National newspaper journalists profess great disdain for any other sort. Television and radio reporters are deemed to have sold out for the lucre and ephemeral fame; magazine journalists are not regarded as 'proper' journalists at all; and the greatest contempt is reserved for the great mass of journalists on all provincial papers, whether daily *or* weekly.

Until you get onto a national, you will be an object of contempt to your Fleet Street peers. Once he has whetted his blade during a brief stint on a provincial paper, Backstabber's next priority will be a job in Fleet Street. For that he will first have had to prove his mettle to his bosses on the provincial - the News Editor and the Editor - and, more importantly, to their counterparts on a national paper.

So what makes Backstabber different from the thousands of other provincial journalists also trying to clamber onto the Inter City line to London? He can easily distinguish himself from his colleagues on the local paper. Most of them will be deadbeats. There is the Sports Editor, a bumptious ruddy-faced fellow who once played rugger for the third team of his local side and never lets you forget it; or the Fashion Editor whose exhaustive coverage of leather and plastic items is explained by the discovery that she is clad in black leather from toe to throat and is having an affair (or rather an *affaire*) with the little *gamine* who is ostensibly her secretary. Disregard any threats from the middle-aged chain-smoking crime specialist who is so hand-in-glove with the local police that he always makes the speech at the annual Benevolent Fund Dinner; or from the Diary writer who spends all her time chatting up members of the Young Farmers' Club and whose only interest is in finding a suitable match before time runs out; or likewise from the Local Government correspondent who is angling for the much more lucrative post of Public Relations Officer for the council and therefore never writes a controversial word about the councillors, regardless of any scandal, however blatant.

At first, there is no alternative to being the office toady. Backstabbing must wait. Be first to arrive in the mornings and last to leave in the evenings. Wear a bleeper at all times and be on call permanently - you might get first shot at covering some of the best stories coming in. File your copy early (do not write 500 words if they have asked for 200, or vice versa). Dress can be a real problem. In the morning you may want to look smart for interviewing the slick local Tory MP, while in the afternoon you will want to be in denim jacket and jeans to talk to the homeless who have been evicted from their hostel by a heartless landlord. If the News Editor insists on a suit and tie being worn in the office, leave the top button undone and tie hanging askew. Once you have reached Fleet Street, a rather more *rechêrché* scruffiness is customary to show that you are indifferent about your looks, particularly when out on jobs where you meet the rest of the 'pack' (other journalists on the same story). Thus the ability to make quick changes in the loo on your way out to cover stories becomes as essential as remembering your notebook and pencil.

GETTING THE COPY

Even the most junior reporter on the smallest weekly paper knows that the first and foremost task of journalism is to get 'stories'. Although the bulk of these - the council meetings, the local soccer fixtures, the Women's Institute monthly debates - come in automatically, the best are found or bought. Provincial newspapers cannot afford chequebook journalism, so 'contacts' are all-important. The odd pint bought for the local police constable, the couple of quid overtly dropped onto the vicar's collection plate, or the racing tips from the Sports Desk regularly passed on to the doorman at the Town Hall will reap their rewards and help build up an invaluable network of contacts. Be generous, and they will ensure that the story is exclusive, and not released instead to rival newspapers.

The very best stories involve people - 'Where's the people angle?' is the News Editor's ceaseless plea. The brightest boys and girls - though it is often better to be a boy in this very sexist profession - learn the ropes on provincial papers then gravitate swiftly to the 'sexy' beats (the most likely areas for good stories and splashes such as crime, politics and the Royals).

The main problem is extracting the story from the person who has it: the wife whose husband has just been chopped into mincemeat at the dog food factory, or the mother of the girl who has just been raped by a gang of drug-crazed youths. Not surprisingly, they may be extremely unwilling to speak to the Press. Reporters who master the art of prising confidences from reluctant witnesses will quickly find themselves whisked to Fleet Street. Here Backstabber gets ahead of the pack.

First he will find out where the potential interviewees live, which is where contacts will prove invaluable. Will that nice policeman check on his computer for the address of the owner of that 'lump of bloody, twisted metal' which used to be a car? Will your mate at the council consult the housing records to find out where the poor wife lives? Then comes the nasty bit - the doorstep 'Hello, I'm from the *Abergavenny Express* and I'd like to say how terribly sorry . . . ' SLAM. That won't do at all. What about the foot-in-the-door approach? 'We won't be more than a minute, but could you just tell me how your husband . . . ' SLAM. Subterfuge is far more likely to succeed - 'I'm from the Health and Safety Executive, and I'd like to discuss with you how your husband happened to fall into the 20-tonne vat of dogmeat . . . '. 'Oh, all right then.' If there is already a 'pack' slavering outside the unfortunate victim's home, then greater subterfuge is called for. There is the Mr Nice and Mr Nasty routine: Backstabber gets a colleague to bang on the door and raise a hullabaloo. When the victim eventually emerges, mouthing obscenities, Backstabber quickly steps forward, flashes his NUJ press card and says smoothly 'I'm from the National Union of Journalists and I understand that the press has been bothering you for several days. We are doing an investigation into abuses of this sort and I wonder if you would like us to help?' The vastly relieved punter replies - 'Not 'arf, come in' - and within half an hour Backstabber will be telephoning in the (for once) genuinely exclusive copy.

NEWSHOUND SNIFFING OUT A JUICY STORY

SOME MORE IDEAS FOR OBTAINING STORIES, AND THEIR MEANINGS

'We want to tell the story through your eyes' (We'll put whatever words we want into your mouth)

'Haven't you noticed the new positive, caring image of our paper?' (We're still going to slag you off once we have the story)

'Have a drink. It'll help you get over the tragedy' (. . . and forget exactly what it was that you said to the press)

'It's important that we get the facts absolutely right' (I want all the salacious bits so that I can ignore the facts and stick to the smut)

'You don't want to believe what people say about this paper' (You certainly can't believe anything you read in it)

GETTING TO FLEET STREET

Two or three years on a provincial paper will be quite enough (after that anyone will be as typecast as Ken Barlow). Backstabber will have already attracted the attention of Fleet Street News Editors by proving to be a source of good stories. One way of gaining this reputation is to be at the printers when the paper is being 'put to bed'. Then Backstabber can steal all the best stories by ringing them through to the News Editors on the national papers. The provincial Editor may wonder how all the paper's best scoops keep appearing in the *Daily Mail* or the *Sun* on the same day, but the Fleet Street hacks will be sufficiently impressed to offer Backstabber the odd shift at holiday time. Should the other local hacks become suspicious, he should immediately initiate rumours about *them* and *their* London contacts in order to throw everyone off the scent.

Backstabber may be tempted to consider becoming a television journalist - a job which may, at first sight, seem more glamorous but which is considered by the Fleet Street diehards to be strictly for those with the concentration span of a gnat. Television reporters are rarely given the chance to report on a subject for more than a couple of minutes, and the coverage is always dominated by its pictorial impact rather than the merit of the story. Television is full of young flighty types - good-looking, young, without commitments, young, uninterested in depth or detail, snappy dressers and - above all - young. They may become famous but, with their Bucks Fizz mentality, they are over the hill by the time they are 35.

There are plenty of other non-Fleet Street options - publications to cover every field of human endeavour, from *Cabinet Maker Monthly* to *Garbage* (the magazine of the rubbish industry). One could, for example, be roach correspondent on the *Angling Times* (or on *Cannabis Monthly* for that matter), but Backstabber will probably not find enough scope here to exercise his talents.

Thus, Fleet Street is the place to be. The nationals are divided into the tabloids (or 'pops'), and the rather grandly self-titled 'qualities' (staffed by people who see themselves as intellectuals, and called 'unpopular' by the tabloid editors). You must decide which group is for you. Once labelled as either a tabloid or a quality journalist, you are unlikely to be able to swap over.

THE TABLOIDS

.. and downmarket Sunday papers want brash young people with few (sorry - no) scruples and no politics, apart from knee-jerk right-wing reactions. The only essential qualification is the ability to prise stories out of people. The final copy bears little relationship to what was written, once it has been through the meat mincer of News Editors, Subs, Revise Subs, Chief Subs, rewrite men (nearly always men), and possibly the Editor as well. Compulsory dress for men is a trench coat, flash suit, featureless tie, and well-worn black shoes (to show that you are used to trailing the streets). Women must display their attributes to even get a look-in (trousers and loose-fitting clothes are definitely out).

THE QUALITIES

.. and their Sunday equivalents seem to suffer from a collective schizophrenia when recruiting staff: they want brash young people who will be able to get exclusives, as well as the pseudo-academic pipe-smoking types who provide reams of worthy copy but who would not recognise a door if it slammed in their face. So they tend to employ people who they hope can do both jobs, but who in reality are incapable of doing either. The qualities take themselves *very* seriously. As for their journalists - they are buskers just like anyone else, writing stories incredibly fast on topics about which they know nothing. The only prerequisite to get a job on a quality is to develop a good line in bullshit - to mug up on the latest economic figures and saucy court cases and be able to talk with equal facility about both.

Backstabber knows that the key to getting a job on Fleet Street is persistence. When he receives the inevitable reply from a News Editor of a national newspaper saying 'Thanks, but no thanks. But please contact us with your story ideas', that is exactly what he does. He clutches the straw. He buys every provincial paper he can find and rings up the News Desk early each day with ideas he has culled. He pesters them with ideas until they take a story, or offer him a shift. Then he begins the climb up the greasy pole.

ON THE STREET

As a newly-fledged national newspaper reporter, Backstabber must get his name in the paper as often as possible. The more times his name appears, the more likely he is to be noticed by the Editor (and his mother will love it). Generally speaking, quantity, not quality, is what counts. Here are some tips:

1. When writing a story with other journalists, Backstabber offers to do the 'pulling together' of the final version of the story. When they adjourn to their favourite pub, he stays behind and knocks all the other names off the story and gives himself the by-line. When they complain the next day, he blames it on the Subs, saying he has already given the Subs a bollocking. (The Subs will do anything for a pint!)

2. Backstabber generates his own stories, otherwise he will get palmed off with the News Editor's - or worse, the Editor's - bad ideas. (If stuck with an Editor's story to do, kill it fast: go to the library and sift through some old cuttings, then go back to him with 'Did you know the story's already been done ages ago by . ')

3. Backstabber gets in early every day. The Press Association (PA) issues a list of stories it is covering and he runs through these on his computer, picks the best story on the day's list and suggests to the News Editor that he covers it. This ensures that Backstabber is on hand for those early-morning disasters such as commuter train crashes and IRA bombs which will guarantee a front page by-line. Turning up late offers others the chance to display their own backstabbing skills. One hapless reporter on a Manchester evening newspaper came in late one day and told the News Editor his alarm clock had broken. His boss's reply was succinct: 'That's all right, laddie. You get yourself a new alarm clock and we'll get ourselves a new reporter.'

4. If all else fails, steal stories from freelance journalists. Once Backstabber has made it to Fleet Street, he can ring up his old paper and tell his erstwhile mates to tip him the wink when a

good tale comes up. They will be delighted to oblige. He gets the News Desk secretary to slip them a pound or two each time (rather less than the going rate, of course). The News Editor will never know where the stories came from. Meanwhile Backstabber tells his old colleagues - who are all anxious for Fleet Street jobs - that he will 'Put in a good word for them and make sure the News Editor knows who the source was'.

THE SUNDAYS

These are probably the most vicious newspapers to work on. For three, four or five days of the working week there is virtually nothing to do. There are too many chiefs and not enough Indians. One excellent Backstabber on a Sunday paper, who happens to 'drink' with his Editor, earns £50,000 a year for editing just one page (badly) each week. (Real Backstabbers employ the time plotting against their rivals and working out how to get rid of the Editor before the Editor gets rid of them.) Then on Friday and Saturday, all hell is let loose: there are stories to cover, scandal to rake up and facts to make up.

Unlike reporters on the dailies (who have six papers to write for each week), on a Sunday writers only get one bite at the cherry. So if a reporter falls out with his News Editor, his life can be made pure hell: he may be despatched on useless stories at the beginning of each week, never to be heard from again. He may even get sent on stories with another reporter - having to do all the work, while the other writer gets the by-line. And it will be another seven days before the next Sunday.

TELLING STORIES

Backstabber reporters on a tabloid will always go for Royal stories. These have one great advantage - they are totally uncheckable. If it is reported that the Queen ate some local housewife's cakes for tea yesterday, nobody will ever deny the story - especially if it appears in a local paper. On Fleet Street, Royal stories are known as 'Fairy Tales' because no-one ever takes them seriously. But readers lap them up - and no prizes for guessing whose by-line will be forever appearing on the front page!

Inventing stories need not be confined to Royal ones, but other sorts can entail the major disadvantage of whacking great libel damages. Libel suits are for the rich and powerful, not the man on the Merton minibus. This makes him an easy target: consequently the tabloids are full of stories about obscure people having sex with their mother, grandmother or pet rabbit. Even the tabloids tend to avoid the famous since the Elton John case, when *The Sun*'s accusations linking the pop star with rent boys were proved wrong. It cost the paper £1 million in damages, and the first 'splash' in history to consist of an apology: the headline ran 'Sorry, Elton!'

Politicians are considered fair game - particularly those in power. To them, any publicity is good publicity. They rarely retaliate unless the libel is so far-fetched ('PM had three prostitutes in one night') that they simply cannot avoid suing you. Lawyers are supposed to advise on libel, but actually the Editor has the final word - which means that if there is a good enough case to argue (or a good enough story) the Editor may choose to ignore the lawyer's counsel.

COMMUNICATION

All journalists must make sure of their lines of communication. It is no good finding yourself in possession of your best-ever story if you have no way of sending it back to your newspaper. If no official channels are available, then Backstabber will make his own arrangements (and if in pursuit of a real scoop, he will not hesitate to sabotage his rival's).

According to Peter Chippindale and Chris Horrie in the unauthorised biography of *The Sun*, both *The Star* and *The Sun* managed to get 'snatch' pictures of Princess Diana on a small Caribbean island, wearing a bikini when she was five months pregnant. The *Sun* reporters found a wire machine on the island and promptly flashed the pictures through, then their Editor allegedly told them to drop an axe onto the machine after they had finished transmitting.

It is not the first reporter on the scene who wins, but the first one to get the story back to the office. Before the days of portable telephones, sabotage was quite simple. The telephone box was an easy target - either with a pair of scissors or, more simply, by getting your office to call you back and then leave the line open, making it impossible for anyone else to get a dialling tone. Backstabber would then saunter out saying to the next reporter waiting in line 'It doesn't work, mate. I've been trying for ages'. These days he has to be a little more technical - spill a cup of tea onto his rival's computer - that should melt their megabytes. Alternatively (for the really unscrupulous), most lap-top computers have a little switch as the back which erases *all* the memory: wait until the opposition is not looking and . . . flick it!

TIME TO FLY

Backstabber journalist likes nothing better than a challenge to keep him up to the mark, so shortly after he has arrived in Fleet Street, to prevent boredom, he will think about a move. Again, there is a career choice: is it to be Editor of a national newspaper, or to become a provincial newspaper Editor, loved and respected in Penny Hasset but unknown anywhere else?

Whatever the aim, Backstabber must ingratiate himself with his immediate bosses. He will go and drink with them and listen to their tedious tales about 'When I was on the road with old Harry, and in those days . . . ', and use the opportunity to glean information about their private lives and past misdemeanours. There used to be a couple of pubs and wine bars (like El Vino's) in and around Fleet Street which were the haunt of all journalists, and where you could meet executives from other papers and find out what vacancies were coming up. Now, with the national press spread between Kensington High Street and Wapping, gossip is much harder to come by. News Editors, stuck behind their desks all day long, are always partial to a convivial pint. Never fail to accept if they invite you along. The trick is to pretend that you are one of the boys, while making sure that you don't get plastered and reveal what you think of the bastards.

Backstabber will readily appreciate the necessity of buttering up the newspaper proprietor. If he unearths any unsavoury dirt on the Editor - or some other senior executive - he will wait until the proprietor next drops in (Maxwell actually flies in by helicopter), then mosey up to him and drop a quiet word in his ear. The ploy *might* backfire and Backstabber could be the one who gets the boot - but nothing ventured, nothing gained - and Backstabber's unerring nose for the most vulnerable spot to stab should obviate most misjudgements. And should the hint bear fruit, he will almost certainly be in line for promotion.

When angling for promotion, you will inevitably meet invisible barriers. You must 'fit in'. On a quality newspaper, that means public school, Oxbridge, an attractive (i.e. fancied by the boss) wife, sober suits, the right connections, and preferably a BBC accent. An obsequious enthusiasm for playing cricket (badly - so you do not outshine the Editor) is often the best qualification.

On the tabloids the complete opposite is required: 'sarf' London background, left school at 16 (without qualifications and preferably under a cloud), trendy suits, loud ties, a marked propensity for swearing, and a nascent beer gut which you try to work off at squash sessions before work.

Backstabber will also consider it well worth becoming 'Father' or 'Mother' (i.e. shop steward) of the NUJ chapel. He will get to know the management and will be in an excellent position to sell all his 'brothers' down the river by agreeing to management demands. Then . . surprise, surprise! . . six months later he lands a plum job as Literary Editor (even if he has never read a book in his life).

SNAKES AND LADDERS

In many ways, being a reporter is in itself the best job since you get the fun of going out into the big wide world, the glory of having your name in the paper, and - as you gain more experience - you are largely your own boss. Many of your associates tied to desk jobs nurture a venomous hatred for you, for they are all too well aware that they have sold their souls for the lolly and lost out on all the fun.

Paradoxically, if you want power, money and a big car you must make the sacrifice and opt for a desk job. You will be called

Assistant Features Editor or Deputy News Editor. One way to speed progress up the ladder is to try and induce other executives to commit professional suicide. On *The Daily Mail* a few years ago, three senior employees agreed that if a particular person were appointed Deputy Editor, they would all resign in protest. A few months later, when the new appointment was announced, the most foolhardy charged into the Editor's office and handed in his letter of resignation. On his way out, he met his two co-conspirators and said 'Well, what about our pact?' To which they both echoed 'Pact? What pact?'

Another possible route is to become a specialist - on crime, the environment, health or politics. If there are no obvious vacancies, create one. Choose the subject of the specialist who is least rated by the News Desk. Get hold of the relevant trade magazines, then first thing the next morning go to the News Editor and offer him the best two or three ideas for stories. As different trade magazines come out on different days, you will soon come to be regarded as the bright young thing who ought to take over the job. Step one up the ladder.

As a specialist, you are supposed to be in competition with your rivals on other papers. This is pure fiction. In fact Backstabber needs to be in league with his co-specialists in the same field so that they can trade stories. No-one wants to be caught out by a News Editor coming up and saying 'I see the *Guardian*'s got a good story in it today. How come we didn't have it?' However, when it comes to a real exclusive Backstabber will not play quite fair, and will make sure he keeps some tasty morsels for himself.

At this stage Backstabber could, if feeling lazy, even return to the provinces. Once he has been 'blooded' on Fleet Street, he can apply for quite senior jobs outside London. But always guard against 'career snakes', down which the unwary can slide to the bottom. Editors and other senior executives are rarely sacked: instead they are found such jobs as Assistant Editor (Special Projects) or Managing Editor (Supplements), with an office, a secretary and a blank desk. If they don't die of boredom, they are weeded out during the next series of cutbacks. Be wary: these non-jobs can be presented in a very attractive way - 'Look, old chap, we've been thinking for a while about Europe and how we really ought to be involved, and we think you're just the right man to help us. You speak French, don't you? Only a little?... well, it doesn't matter. You see, we want to draw up a policy that will drag us screaming into the Twenty-first Century ... '. Before you know it, you will be upstairs with the rest of the dead wood.

THE VIEW FROM THE TOP

Number One in the newspaper world is the Editor (not to be confused with the Managing Editor, the Deputy Editor, the Editorial Director or the Chief Sub Editor). Although the Publisher is sometimes the more important figure, it is generally the Editor (occasionally known as 'Editor-in-Chief') who is the boss. To become Editor, you must not be squeamish about backstabbing and undermining your colleagues whenever necessary.

Once Backstabber is at the top table and has gained his entrée into the editorial conferences, he can start sniping at the existing Editor. If the paper's circulation is going up, initiate a stream of special projects - such as book extracts (qualities), games (tabloids), or colour supplement health and fitness features (a winner in either) - then claim the credit for the rise in sales. If the circulation is falling, generate nasty rumours by commissioning market researchers to discover the reason why, followed up by internal memos to the proprietor detailing your findings. If all else fails, leak bogus information to other newspapers' media correspondents.

Backstabber should have no difficulty inheriting the newly-vacated job. But does he really want it? Some Fleet Street papers get through Editors almost as fast as football clubs get through managers. They can be sacked for printing pictures of Prince Willy's Harry (or is it the other way round?), or for *failing* to print them. Other papers hang onto their Editors for so long that they become atrophied and fit only for retirement.

As Editor, Backstabber will have to tolerate his publisher interfering and pestering him on the telephone every day, trying to ensure that his friends get a good show. One long-standing Sunday newspaper Editor, interviewed about his relationship with the owner, tried to stress how independent he was. Very convincing he was, too, until the camera crew asked for some general shots of him working at his desk - at which point he picked up the telephone, pretended he was calling the owner and said 'It's Ron here. Just wanted to check the front page was okay.' The entire proceedings were screened to the watching millions on television.

Nor need the Editor expect to get the blame solely for falling circulation. If it goes *up*, the proprietor may start to moan about the fact that the extra print costs outweigh the revenue from additional sales; and he will always be standing there, ogre-like, grousing about this or that editorial or splash. Moreover, there will be a steady stream of law suits whenever the journalists libel their subjects.

So why does anyone want to be Editor? Because they want to be BOSS - the hub of the paper, its lynch pin. They can pull out any story they don't like, instruct journalists to write on any subject they fancy, enjoy numerous free holidays on all sorts of spurious grounds, and boast the biggest and best set of wheels in the car park.

And to cap it all, no more covert knifing. Now Backstabber can revel in the full-frontal plunge of the dagger into upstart executives and bumptious journalists. But always with a care for his own suits - blood stains are so hard to remove!

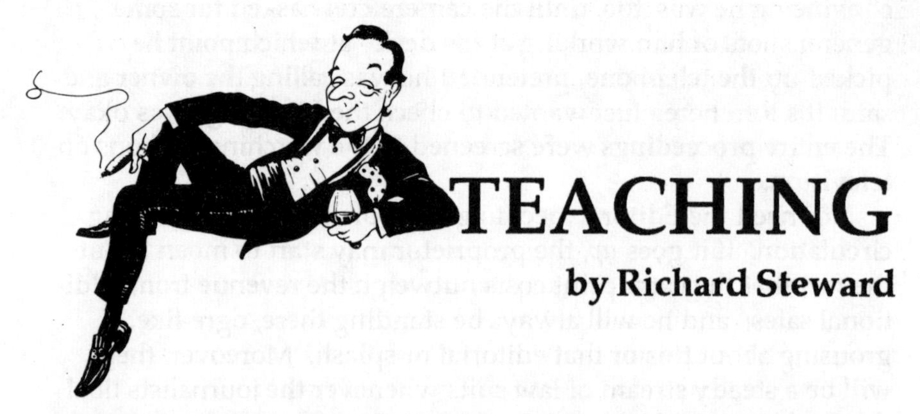

TEACHING

by Richard Steward

HEADING FOR THE HEAD'S CHAIR

'Do I have to go to school today, Mother? Everybody hates me. The teachers hate me, the children hate me, even the caretaker hates me!'

'Yes, dear, you must. After all, you are the Headmaster.'

It goes without saying that anyone who sets out deliberately to join the teaching profession is insane. Most Teachers would rather be doing something else: training to be astronauts, climbing Mount Everest, or baking cakes for the W.I. winter jamboree. Many have taken the job as a last resort, having been rejected by the Civil Service, various insurance agencies and every double-glazing company within a thirty-mile radius. So, almost overnight, fledgling Teachers discover a vocation, a worthwhile job, and condemn themselves to standing in front of rows of screaming desks for the next thirty or forty years.

The committed Backstabber Teacher - more interested in raw ambition than money (Teachers do not believe in money, never having seen it!) - can soon have the world of education at his or her feet. However, those wishing to rise to the top must bear one or two points in mind before they can relax in the only comfortable chair in the school - the one in the Head's office:

1. Teachers are universally despised - even by other Teachers. Everyone has been to school and everyone can remember nasty old Scrogget who used to nail heads to the desk by hammering tin-tacks through pierced ears, or the vast Miss Bullivant who was famed for her habit of scorching miscreants with her garlic and pickled onion breath.

2. Teachers are expected to know everything. For some, this is a natural gift: they can talk knowledgeably on any subject for any given length of time without knowing the first thing about it. Others find it more difficult, and the true Backstabber quickly develops strategies for gathering 'useful' information (which common sense normally suggests is totally useless) or learns to lie with conviction.

3. Teaching is not a career - it is a profession. This means that you must never admit to wanting to get on: you are in it for the children, not for yourself. Money does not concern you, and even if the bank is threatening to repossess your house, sell the clothes off your back and put your wife on the streets, you must never be so unprofessional as to ask for a rise or for promotion. You love it, don't you!

4. Teachers care. They care about everything from Sally Slaprash's holiday plans to the tragic tale of Timmy the hamster's fall into the waste-disposal unit. And they still have time to consider seriously all the bright ideas emanating from the armchair educationalists at County Hall. Never let it be said that it was you who did not listen when Kylie - acned, prepubescent and destined to become the school's youngest mother - asked about 'them thingies what you get from the chemist', or that it was you who laughed when the Senior Adviser on Something-Important-that-Nobody-Quite-Understands proposed a county-wide project exploring ways to teach mathematics without using numbers.

THE FIRST STEPS

Teachers have to be trained, and the ambitious Backstabber is advised to seek out one of the trendier teacher training colleges. These may be distinguished by the number of times they are vilified in the media and branded as liberal lunatic asylums. To get accepted as a trainee you need only enthusiasm and commitment (a slight disability also helps, or a history of political persecution, or - best of all - a partial knowledge of English). But if you are decidedly run-of-the-mill you will have to rely on fanatical devotion to new ideas. Above all, remember to mention children as often as possible. This may sound obvious, but in high-powered discussions about education they are often forgotten. Of course, at a later stage in your career they can be forgotten completely but, as a beginner, it is wise to bear them in mind.

Teaching practice is the most important element of the course. It does not take long and is not complicated. Remember that you will probably be observed in action in front of a class only once or twice - usually by a drunk who cannot remember your name anyway - and told that your lesson was well-planned and exciting but you ought to do something about the colour of your sandwich box. The only way you can fail teaching practice is to die in the classroom. This happens occasionally - usually as a result of some minor misunderstanding involving a disturbed pupil and a shotgun.

CHOOSING A SCHOOL

Armed with a teaching certificate, you are ready to launch yourself into the fray. A good choice of school is essential. Here are a few of the types you are likely to encounter:

THE INNER CITY COMPREHENSIVE - Offers free accommodation, help with your mortgage and reduced teaching time. None of this compensates for the fact that your first encounter with a class may resemble a clash with a band of international pirates. However, if you escape with minor injuries (just the odd scar or acid burn) you could become Head of Department within a year.

THE RURAL GRAMMAR SCHOOL - Here the staff rarely stir unless you sit in their chair or use their coffee mug. You can slip into a comfortable routine, whiling away endless hours in the staffroom dreaming nostalgically of cucumber sandwiches and cricketing triumphs of yesteryear. Staff meetings are conducted in Latin and the most important event on the scholastic calendar is the Remembrance Day Service - long live the Empire! On Prize Day, everyone gets a prize and the Headmaster congratulates his staff on their educational prowess in getting the top one percent of children through their GCSE's. After a year in a grammar school you are finished, happy to wallow in tea-time excellence until you retire.

THE PUBLIC SCHOOL - A haven for old school ties who worship tradition and enjoy life's pleasures, such as meals at the Headmaster's table, bringing your dog into work, and cricket matches that monopolise the school timetable. Turning up for lessons is rather a bore, but you usually manage to finish the *Daily Telegraph* by lunchtime. One thing is certain: you need never worry about new-fangled innovations - public schools are exempt from change. Nevertheless, the public school offers interesting possibilities for the social-climbing Backstabber. Extra tuition for Lady Letitia could provide your entrée to aristocratic circles and stately homes up and down the country. However, masters who impregnate a deb or mistresses who seduce the senior wrangler may find difficulty maintaining employment.

THE MIDDLE CLASS COMPREHENSIVE - The perfect choice for the ambitious Backstabber. The large number of staff will ease the progress of your rapid promotion, and the reasonable range of pupils will present few problems once you have learnt to ignore them successfully. Such establishments offer all the facilities you will need on your way to the top: a computer room so that you can familiarise yourself with the latest technology (in order to mystify others with it later), squash courts (for informal games with senior staff), sufficient secretarial staff (so no-one realises how many personal letters go out on school writing paper), and - above all - a large staff noticeboard which you must cover as quickly as possible with important memoranda bearing your name. This kind of school enables you to establish yourself quickly and gain a reputation as a go-ahead type who is 'terribly efficient' and 'terribly good with the children'.

THE INTERVIEW

Once you have chosen an appropriate school, compile a *curriculum vitae* and an enthusiastic letter of application. If you claim to be an amateur tree-surgeon or a part-time shark fisherman, make sure you know what you are talking about: it is always possible that one of the Governors had a bit part in 'Jaws' or likes to do all his own pollarding. Admittedly it is not likely, but then neither is finding a Governor who knows anything about education. Be on your guard.

An interview for a teaching job is a barbaric affair. Usually four or five candidates are called and together they endure a day of tours, talks, friendly chats and informal interviews. Throughout the ordeal, they are obliged to pretend that they are enjoying it all immensely and that they get on well with their rivals for the post. The main thought in your mind - as you sit ignored in the staffroom - is the fervent hope that all four rival candidates may suddenly drop dead, conveniently eliminating your competition. As all the other candidates will be thinking exactly the same thing, you should assume an air of superiority, smile smugly and give the impression that the job is already yours.

The formal interview occurs at the end of the day, when you will be ushered into the Head's office for an SS-style interrogation. Your c.v. will be thoroughly dissected and your commitment explored to the limits. You will also be asked about your 'other interests'. Beware! - this is the most dangerous part of the interview. At the time you may profess a keen desire, say, to run the school hockey team, but you must *never* commit yourself to anything particular: you may find yourself in charge of the under-thirteens' Christian Union!

You will, of course, be well prepared for questions on innovations in education, but beware the Governor's question: they generally have only one, but they have used it for years and it is guaranteed to confound every candidate. Governors come in a wide variety of shapes and sizes. Parent Governors are generally interested in the school, so their influence is minimal and they should not be taken too seriously. The potential nightmare is Major General Hackenthorpe, who thinks the school is an Eton or Harrow and whose only interest is in the bottle of whisky he has spotted imperfectly concealed by a row of books on sex education behind the Head's desk. Likely to be asleep for most of the interview, he will wake up with a startled look and suddenly ask if you think it is advisable to teach Latin to horses: laughing will lose you the job, but discussing horses in the context of the National Curriculum will impress him immensely, earn you a friend for life, and the job will be in the bag.

A NOTE ON THE ARCHETYPAL BACKSTABBER

Backstabbers in teaching are not in it for the fame, the riches or the prestige. These assets do not exist in the teaching profession (the only notorious Teachers are the those hauled up before the beak accused of interfering with little boys). Backstabbers are in it because of a desire to wield power over others. Many will have had bad experiences themselves with teachers when young (the Scrogget syndrome again) and now wish to turn their pain onto others with the same sado-masochistic fervour. It will not surprise you to learn that the most effective Backstabbers are often single, with weird fetishes and curious hobbies. These people are easily recognised in the staffroom: they rarely sit still and generate an air of ceaseless industry, yet their clothes remain immaculately pressed and even their hair shouts 'Look at me, I'm perfect'. Recognise yourself?

THE FIRST JOB

It is always wise to adopt a low profile for the first few weeks, thus giving yourself the chance to survey the scene, identify weaknesses and strengths, look for openings, and - above all - work out who are the people to watch. Try not to let anyone know that this is your first job. The Head is likely to have forgotten so it should be fairly easy to convince everyone that you have all the experience necessary. This gives you immediate authority, though you should be careful not to lose it by asking too many naïve questions or complaining about the classes you have been allotted. You can find out all you need to know from the pupils or the caretaker, and you should become fully informed about everything that goes on in the place as quickly as you can.

At this stage in your career the children are actually useful, and by dint of a few threats and bribes you can get an enormous amount of information out of them regarding the way the school operates. Children always know who is the real boss and they are particularly good at unearthing juicy bits of gossip which will enable you to blackmail colleagues at a later date. It is essential to give the impression of professional discretion, so when Damian and Jade are gleefully telling you about Mrs Dogberry's husband, the dachshund and the rubberware, it is vital that you feign indifference and mild disapproval. As soon as the class gets a whiff of disapproval, or of moral rectitude, they will be off like greyhounds, regaling you with all sorts of carnal and criminal activity: the Head had to resign because of Tracy in the sixth form .... Mr Firelighter keeps a bottle of scotch in his desk drawer .... don't ever go into the stock cupboard with Creepy Hedges .... and so on. All this information should be catalogued and recorded on your card index or computer database - it will be *very* useful later.

Most Teachers are clearly recognisable 'types', and in the first few weeks it will become obvious into which categories the different members of staff fall. The following guide, used in conjuction with your staff dossier, should enable you to identify them with ease. Also included are hints and tips on how to deal with them effectively.

THE EAST EUROPEAN DICTATOR

This is a character you are likely to encounter at once. He will be wearing a faded tweed jacket, an old school tie, a V-neck sweater and jackboots. He does not talk, he lectures - and he does not care whether you are listening or not. He always has something to complain about and he objects to everything. Nothing is done in the school without his say so. He is particularly opposed to fun and any attempt at humour in the staffroom will be severely frowned upon. Above all, he hates children. He force-feeds them education in the same way that farmers force-feed pigs. He is not interested in making the lessons interesting for the class, only effective. When members of staff gather in huddles to discuss the miserable old bastard, someone will always leap to his defence with the phrase 'Ah, but he gets good results'. (But so does the rack!)

The best way to deal with him is to ignore him completely. He will not mind and may well think more of you for doing so. Dictators are always bachelors who - having been tyrannised by their mothers or by bigger boys in school - feel the need to dominate in their turn. As a result they have hobbies which give them scope to dictate - shooting, war games, train sets, etc. If you can find out which of these he most enjoys, his objections to anything can be diffused with a few well-chosen words: 'I understand you like trains . . . '. At that, his eyes will will light up with a fanatical gleam, he will promptly become chief signalman and drop any further pretence of educational authority.

THE EAST EUROPEAN DICTATOR

The Dictator's female counterpart is very similar - the tweed jacket and the jackboots are standard issue - but she completes the outfit with a striking summer dress and a sharpened umbrella. Keen on hunting, you will probably find that she runs a vicar somewhere, or dominates the local council - a veritable Valkyrie in winceyette.

THE WIDE-EYED INCOMPETENT

You may not get time talk to the Incompetent for several months, but you will be very aware of his presence. Your first meeting will be heralded by a scuffling at the staffroom door, followed by a swirl of activity and a flurry of papers and exercise books. He will charge in like a tornado and attempt to talk to at least three people at once, relating a garbled account of fighting children, broken furniture, missed appointments, mislaid reports and desperate misunderstandings. While long-suffering colleagues endeavour to find his keys - he is always losing his keys - he will race to the photocopier and copy everything in sight, including his tie, his driving licence (in case he loses it) and his plan for the next lesson. The discovery of his keys (marking his place in a publication entitled *How To Cope With Stress*) will divert him from his task and send him hurtling across the room to rescue them. When the bell goes, he will leap to his feet like a crazed monkey whose tail has just been connected to the national grid and charge out of the room. Two minutes later he will reappear, even more flustered, to retrieve the lesson plan abandoned on the photocopier.

WIDE-EYED AND INCOMPETENT

The Incompetent does not have to be dealt with, just avoided. If you are unlucky enough to find that he is your Head of Department you must take action immediately. You must assume control and - although you may be tied up for weeks looking for his keys - you will be in line for his job when he finally cracks. The

Incompetent's crack-up is a spectacular event: he will charge in, screaming at the top of his voice and shouting foul obscenities at invisible green gnomes. He will then proceed to rip up everything within reach and hurl himself around the room, bouncing from chair to chair with increasing velocity. Finally, he will turn on his faithful friend, the photocopier, and attempt to eat it - photocopying himself in the process - before collapsing and sobbing bitterly into the curtains.

The female Incompetent is precisely the same, although you may remark a tendency to converse with the plants at times of extreme stress.

THE ART TEACHER

You probably will not realise for some time that the Art Teacher is a teacher at all. Dressed like a '60's glove puppet, he will pop up all over the place when you least expect him - in the post office, at the bakery, or down by the pool. If you want to find him, don't bother looking in the art room - he is never there. He will probably spend more time in your classes than teaching art, and in many ways he is the most disruptive element in the school. Even head-banger Jason, recognising a superior talent for mischief, will abandon his attempt to dismantle his desk in favour of watching raptly as the Art Teacher systematically destroys your lesson. All nose and whiskers, the man is a menace - the modern equivalent of the all-licensed fool, someone to be enjoyed and encouraged. Beware of his

A 60 S GLOVE PUPPET

bouts of melancholy, caused by the occasional remembrance of his teaching commitments which interfere with his real aim in life - to become a great artist.

The female Art Teacher is an equal menace: what *he* does with buffoonery, *she* does with exaggerated gestures and operatic swoons. She is a figure of towering excellence and her talents, darlings, are limitless. Dressed like a Pre-Raphaelite pixie, she will flounce in and out of your lessons demanding to be admired and courted. Critical of everything, she stirs everybody up: but that does not matter - she is secure in the knowledge of her own greatness.

THE MATRON-IN-WAITING

Easily recognised by the size of her bust, which expands in direct proportion to her responsibilities, she is definitely a character to watch. She is likely to be as ruthlessly ambitious as any male Backstabber, but much more subtle. She is aiming for a Deputy-Headship, and will achieve it without too much effort. Beware of her encyclopaedic social knowledge: her staff database is likely to be twice as large and twice as dangerous as yours. What is more, your own transgressions are sure to be on it! Best to avoid her - allow her to sail, stately as a galleon, unimpeded to the top. Never attempt to cross her, or enquire as to the exact nature and extent of her responsibilities.

THE TIME-SERVER

Tucked away somewhere in every staffroom are one or two Teachers hanging on until retirement - the dead wood. Disappointed long ago, but clinging onto positions of dubious responsibility, they gaze - glassy-eyed - into the future. They do the bare minimum but, for perverse reasons known only to themselves, hate the fact that anyone else should want to do a thing. A bright idea, chuffing up the track from whatever direction, is sure to be stopped in its tracks by these old buffers. Any career scheme must be skilfully re-routed in order to avoid them.

MATRON-IN-WAITING AND THE TIME SERVER

THE INDIVIDUAL

Yet another easily identified category. Individuals are found in every staffroom in the country, all believing that they are one of a kind and a cut above the rest: there is the Politician (scheming darkly in the corner), the Mad Scientist (adding the finishing touches to a great invention that will never see the light of day), the Vegetarian (wearing ethnic clothes and smelling of herbal poultices), the Sports Master (dressed in sweaty tracksuit, hob-nailed football boots and brimful of smutty jokes), and the Carer (the Mavis Riley of the staffroom, who does not believe in doing anything which might upset anyone: she would never go on strike because it would hurt the children - and besides, her husband has got a good job).

THE IDEAS MAN

This is the real man of the moment - Backstabber's role model. Distinguished by nothing in particular, he is positively rocketing to the top. He wears soft-soled shoes for sneaking up on people in the corridor, his hair is brilliantined so that he can slip unnoticed

IDEAS MAN

through cracks in the door, and his eyes are beady and alert. Like a slug with a stiletto, he is always ready with a witty quip and an oily smile. He knows exactly what he is doing and specialises in everything that is new and trendy. He has a tentacle in every pie and gathers jargon with all the relish and discrimination of a hungry piranha. You will find that he is responsible for Social Education, Records of Achievement, Assessment, Profiling, Economic Awareness - in fact anything that has nothing to do with teaching but promises *power*. He assiduously circulates copies of all his correspondence to ensure everyone knows just how hard he works. He rarely comes into contact with pupils - he is far too important for that - although he prefaces all his proposals with 'It has to be in the children's best interests'.

It is essential to get on the right side of this man - to become his No. 1 henchman. Preliminary overtures should be made via a memo - his principal means of communication - but as you gain his confidence you will be allowed to leave type-written letters on one of his desks. Try to carve out a niche in one of his ideas and support him at every opportunity, so that you are ready to slip greasily into his shoes when he moves on.

The Ideas Woman is just as greasy and just as dedicated. Indeed, in many schools it is hard to be sure whether the source of all great schemes is actually a man or a woman! Sex is not part of their plans - they are far too busy for that.

THE ROUTE TO THE SUMMIT

Once you are settled in a job, you are on the home run. There are just two hurdles to clear - middle management and senior management - before you can claim the comfortable chair. With a sharp knife and dedication it should not take long. Once you have become familiar with your colleagues and your surroundings, you can start promoting yourself at their expense. Begin by offering to help people out, make helpful suggestions to senior staff ('I'd be more than happy to teach Scrogget's Latin classes after school if ever he should think of retiring'), and - best of all - try and gain a reputation as someone willing to deal with troublesome pupils ('I'll have him in my class if he's causing you any bother, old chap').

Backstabber is also a great initiator. Start a few clubs, get lots of people involved, make sure everyone knows you are responsible, and then get some other idiot to take over. Plan a school trip to Togoland (it goes without saying that the only other free place will go to the person who will do all the work for you). Get your name onto the staffroom noticeboard every day, give out important messages, remind people of things they probably know already, gather witty press clippings from the local papers, and thank colleagues profusely for their kind support. Never be seen in front of a class - this may undermine your management potential - but make sure you know the name of every child in the school so you can join in at all the case conferences and say, helpfully, 'He's never any trouble with me'. Above all, be sure to be seen: charge purposefully around with a clipboard and an A4 diary stuffed full of memos, muttering 'I must ring County Hall'. Refer to the Head and the Deputies by their Christian names and associate only with senior staff. Before long, everyone will assume that you are responsible for half the school. As soon as an opportunity for promotion comes up, it will be assumed that the job is yours and your election will be uncontested.

Backstabber is also a great course-goer. Courses are vital for two reasons: firstly, you have to collect a certain number of them, like cards in Monopoly, in order to advance to the next stage in your career; and, secondly, they get you out of the classroom as often as possible. You must sign up for everything - the more ludicrous the better: so although a seminar on *Self-Expression Through Touch and Dance* may not immediately appeal, you will probably find that it is greatly respected and crucial to your professional development. Management courses are a must: there you will role-play important tasks like talking to others, sitting up straight on your chair, finding your keys, adjusting your tie and writing things in your diary. In the welcome moments of relaxation you will be able to consult with Backstabbers from other schools and learn a few new tricks to unleash on your colleagues when you finally get back to work.

As Head of Department you can really stir things up. By now you will have given up doing any original work, but you will have become a past master of passing other people's work off as your own. You will delegate as much as possible to lighten your own load and free you for advanced backstabbing; this may place a burden on your department, but if *you* look busy enough, no-one will notice. Your time in this capacity should be spent preparing yourself for the next great leap - the Deputy-Headship.

As Deputy-Head in charge of curriculum (the pastoral Deputy will be your rival, the Matron-in-Waiting) you will effectively control the school. The Matron will be responsible for making the tea at parents' evenings and showing health education films on menstruation to first-year girls; you will be responsible for everything else. By means of careful manipulation of the timetable you will be able to exercise some hold over every Teacher in the school. The Headmaster may not be interested in anything more complicated than the racing results, so you could be on your own. Using your finely-tuned powers of delegation you will be able to work out a system whereby the school runs itself and you are free to get on with the main task of the aspiring Backstabber leader - good ideas. There is no further need for contact with children at this stage in your career, though you must never forget to reiterate 'It has to be in the children's best interests': you may not have seen a child for weeks (or years, in some cases) but you must remember to acknowledge their existence.

Some Backstabbers are happy to remain at the level of Deputy for the rest of their careers, delighting in their stranglehold over the school and its staff. Many see a Headship as a denial of responsibility and decide to stay on, like spiders in the centre of a vast web, slowly feeding off others and monitoring the pulse of power as it beats along the silken lines of communication. However, the more subtle Backstabber will see the Headship as a chance for a rest - a sabbatical if you like - during which he can recuperate and gather his resources for an assault on the citadel of true power: County Hall.

The move from Deputy to Head Teacher is relatively straightforward if you have orchestrated your attack. As soon as you take up your post in charge of the curriculum, you begin to introduce changes - slowly at first, as if you were merely flexing your muscles, but then faster and faster. Take a leaf out of the Secretary of State for Education's book and introduce complicated, mind-bending schemes which are ultimately unworkable: these you will brandish like medals won in battle before the Board of Governors who interview you for the Headship, to impress upon them what you are capable of. They will see you as a creature of vision, a true leader. The school you leave behind will be in a state of chaos, but you will have proved your credentials as a shaker and a mover - someone fit to lead the school in prayers and exhort them to keep their ties done up.

Having convinced the Board of your power, your commitment and your desire to do everything in the best interests of the children, you can accept the job, retire to your comfortable office, block up the door and relax. As Head Teacher, you may safely ignore not only the children but the staff as well.

THE CHURCH

by Stephan Hopkinson

VIRTUOUS BACKSTABBING, OR HOW TO FEEL GOOD WHEN YOU'RE BEING BAD

The Church is probably the last place you would expect to find Backstabbers. Few of the Clergy would admit - even to themselves - that backstabbing gives them either profit or pleasure. In reality it may well do both, but they prefer to think of it as their moral duty. Thus, if your Curate has rashly crossed your path you may say 'I feel, Bishop, that in conscience I must let you know . . . ' or 'I'm sure that there is some field in which Mr Slope's abilities would find better employment.' In this way you not only appear to act in the 'highest interests' of the victim in particular and of the Kingdom of God in general, but also gain credit for your fearless outspokenness.

The Backstabber Cleric will also chivvy his congregation from time to time in order to keep them up to snuff. Make your point, but cloak your barbs with humour: 'I have tried to reach the poor of this parish and judging by the amount of the collection this Sunday, I have succeeded.'

THE BACKSTABBER AND HIS VICTIM

Within the official or 'trade union' branch of the Church - the ordained ministry - the Backstabber is not hard to detect. He is, above all, a conformist - and his own particular conformity will depend on the school of Churchmanship he has elected to pursue. His targets will be those within that school who appear to threaten his own continued promotion. Their worst offence will be rocking the boat, or any variation from the party line: this misdemeanour can be conveniently highlighted at one of those innumerable groups or committee meetings in which Backstabber delights. A potential rival for a coveted chairmanship can, in his absence, be described as 'Not quite sound, I sometimes fear', or 'Much as I admire Mr/Father/my good friend Arabin, I cannot feel it would be right . . . ' Equally, a neighbouring church which is much better attended than the Backstabber's own, can often be accused of 'using gimmicks'. By this is meant 'Someone else has had an excellent idea, and I wish I'd thought of it first.'

YOUR AMBITION

If you see youself as a future Bishop - a *real* Bishop with a Cathedral (there is no substitute for the True Purple) - you must adhere to the Identikit episcopal ideal: a minor public school for starters and, if possible, Oxbridge (where you can flaunt your hood of scarlet or white.) Should there have been a war in recent years, a bedizened chaplain's scarf also looks admirable (medals are too much to hope for), and some touch of the muscular Christian goes down well - even a half-Blue puts you ahead of the competition. A wife - preferably with a little money of her own - not too well dressed, and certainly not 'flashy' (for which 'attractive' may be read!). If you can get a paperback published (ideally, a recommended Lent book) that is sheer bonus. Otherwise a slot on local radio or even a column in the local newspaper must serve: this is what is known as keeping in touch with the outside world. But not too much in touch - as a Backstabber you will be very careful never to over-express political or social concern.

HINTS TO THE APPRENTICE BACKSTABBER

Since most of us are (a) in the mediocre class, (b) like to have other people's esteem, and (c) like even more to have our own, there exists in each of us the makings of a Backstabber. Often while publicly expressing heartfelt sympathy for the suffering of others, we cannot resist some delicate imputation of their guilt or folly as being responsible for their misfortunes: 'I always said he shouldn't drive so fast . . . ' or 'If only she had been a little less selfish . . . '. But this is mere apprentice stuff. If you are to become really adept as a Backstabber there is a great deal more to learn. The following recommendations should be carefully studied and ruthlessly applied:

1. NEVER allow your self-interest to appear. You should appear to be actively supporting the victim you intend to destroy: 'Of course, I don't believe what they're saying about Tom . . . ' or 'He's one of my best friends, and to say that he's having an affair with a parishioner is ridiculous' (so, in truth, it is, but once you have sown the seed it won't seem so). If by any chance the victim gets to hear of the slander, you can say that you firmly denied a rumour which was circulating.

2. In fact, it is as well NEVER to be too knowledgeable about the matter. This can be difficult, as there is a strong temptation to show oneself as being in the know - 'What actually happened, they tell me, was . . . '. Rather, you should put it all down to that pernicious pterodactyl, the egregious 'little bird', which flies round dropping poison, like Hamlet's uncle, into convenient ears. By disclaiming any personal knowledge, you will maintain the illusion of fairminded disbelief, while making sure the story is perpetuated, and thereby encouraging the really wicked legend that 'There is no smoke without fire'.

3. An ingenious variation of this technique is practised by some writers of autobiography - it not only stabs the designated back but can also wreck a longstanding friendship: 'I well remember the Bishop of Barset saying that the Dean had never been sober since he knew him . . . ' - Splendid!

4. For this reason, NEVER pass on your particular poison under the pledge of secrecy: 'I have it on the best authority - Mrs Barchester herself told me - but of course that's between you, me and

the gatepost.' Secrecy certainly won't be observed and may well be used against you. How much better to put it indirectly: 'Isn't it awful what some people will say? You won't believe it, but there's a wicked rumour that Mr Quiverful hasn't spoken to his wife for a week'.

5. It's much better to go for people's *good* side rather than their soft underbelly. Their weaknesses are so well known already that any additional anecdote is just old hat. Try instead to follow Hitler's rule: let the lie be so outrageous that it simply has to be true. Thus, choir- and scout-masters - not to mention Curates - are always a possible target for: 'I know Mr Thorne does simply splendid work with the boys, but I do sometimes wonder . . .'.

THE ESSENCE OF BACKSTABBING

To summarise, the typical religious (ordained or lay) Backstabber is a person of very moderate abilities, but with ambition far in their excess. This ambition often aims at exalting Backstabber. It 'puts down the mighty from their seat', not necessarily to set Backstabber up there instead, but just to ensure that the seat goes unoccupied - and so make Backstabber feel better as he perches on his own modest footstool. Backstabber does not like other people to succeed, and so will hint at the dishonesty and real unworthiness of any such success. The writer of the Book of Job painted a likeness of Backstabber in the Satan of his opening chapters - although in a very charitable way he allowed the fallen archangel to be a son of God. Satan's purpose was to query the honesty of the supposedly virtuous: 'Are they *really* friends of yours?' he asked the Almighty, 'Or only pretending to be, for what they can get out of it?' So poor Job had to be put through the mill - his family and household suffering along with him - just to thwart Satan's attempted backstab. So too Othello and Desdemona had to die to satisfy Iago's envy of their success in both love and war.

FOR VICTIMS ONLY

The ambitious Backstabber, as described above, is easily recognisable: he's on the way up - in earthly, if not in heavenly terms.

More difficult to detect is the 'Iago' Backstabber. This brand of Backstabber actually *likes* hurting people and demonstrating to himself his secret and destructive skill. In this he resembles a certain type of murderer - it literally makes him feel good, and this job satisfaction supersedes any other consideration. This can be done very simply and pleasantly with the sort of remark that begins 'I'm sure you'd like to know what they are saying . . . ' or 'Let me speak frankly, as an old friend . . . '. Considerable pain can thus be inflicted under the guise of affectionate consideration. On parting, the true Backstabber will be sure to add 'Now don't let this worry you . . . ', thereby assuring a sleepless night for his victim.

Parishioners are also adept at backstabbing and may well turn their skills upon *you*. It would be hard to find a better example than Mrs Proudie. She was a wealthy and pious widow, much courted by the Vicar of the parish, one of whose bountiful stock of six Curates was each day deputed to take tea with her - the Vicar himself went on Sundays. She had undoubtedly, it seemed, murdered her late husband, since every time she spoke his name she would cross herself. If this pious exercise was accidentally omitted, the next mention of his name got a double sanctification (clearly an attempt to appease his hostile spirit). But when she discussed the clergy she wielded her stiletto with unholy gusto: 'I never, as you know, join in gossip - I think it deeply un-Christian and I despise all unkind criticism as a sin. If you can't say anything nice about others, as dear Charles [- *sign of the cross* -] used to maintain, say nothing at all. So if Mr Grantly, your predecessor at All Saints, couldn't keep his fingers out of the collection box, it wasn't really his fault. Having a wife like that - never sober for two days at a time - would try the patience of a saint. So we won't talk about him any more, lest I say something uncharitable.'

Or, parishioners may indulge in wistful recollection:

- 'Ah, in dear Mr Harding's time we often had chairs in the aisles at Evensong; but then, he was a wonderful preacher . . . '; or

- 'Such a pity your wife isn't interested in the Sunday School. I always say . . . ' (you bet she does); or

- 'How clever of you, Vicar, to find that delightful Curate. It's such a pleasure to hear the Service beautifully sung . . . ' (implication: 'At last!').

It is conversations of this sort, no doubt, that lead to the barely-veiled dislike felt by many Incumbents for their predecessors. Nothing is harder to accept with cheerful charity than lavish praise for a predecessor, with its implied diminution of oneself.

Once aware that Backstabber is at work, there are counter-measures which can be taken to defuse the planted bombs:

1. If you think you have identified your attacker - or if you have very good reason for suspicion - you can retaliate by using his or her own weapons. Thus, in conversation with others you can remark 'Isn't it sad about dear Eleanor? It's probably the menopause (or 'her not being appointed JP', or the 'trouble she's having with her eldest') that makes her say such catty things. She can't keep her bitterness from coming out'. If necessary this can go further: 'Why, she speaks unkindly even about *you* - and when you think what you've done for that woman . . .'

2. Affect not to know what's being said, but denounce tittle-tattle as a contemptible evil in the parish; do so at some meeting (the Church Council perhaps) at which the source of the trouble is probably among those present. Make a particular point that the mere *listening* to such stories is contaminating, and watch the faces of your audience closely. Those who thank you afterwards for your powerful talk will probably be amongst those who have most enjoyed hearing the scandal, and relished passing it on.

3. Remember that prayer - if conducted in public - is a splendid way of getting your own back. Thus: 'May those who think and speak wicked evil of their neighbours see the light, and come to realise that it is their own secret sin they denounce in others'. Or go on to hint at incipient madness: 'Forgive, O Lord, those whose tongues stray viciously from the truth. Where their minds are already darkening into insanity, grant light and healing, and help

all of us to think of them with pity.'

4. Where Backstabber uses an open approach - intended to sap the victim's self-confidence and generally reduce him to pulp - the approach will probably take the 'I think you ought to hear what everyone is saying about . . .' line suggested above. The best riposte to this is a cheerful 'What are they saying? . . . let them say . . . I don't bother about it anyway'; or else: 'Join the club, you should hear what they are saying about *you*'. In the same way, the really nasty letter clearly intended to hurt should be answered with an infuriating apparent misunderstanding: 'Please don't apologise. I do realise that it was only foolishness on your part, and not pure malice'. The more indignant Backstabber's follow-up to this, the more benevolent should be your supposed attitude. It is a form of soft answer that drives the recipient to suicidal wrath.

5. There is, of course, the possibility of your being a person of such simplicity and niceness that the fiercest stabs are blunted and turn back upon their inflictor. Unfortunately, few of us are lucky enough to find this resource available.

YOUR METHODS

'But how,' you ask yourself, 'How can I make my mark? How do I catch the eye of those powerful secret agents (the patronage secretaries) who will put my name forward to the Lord Chancellor or the Prime Minister? Or even remind the Diocesan Bishop of my existence?'

And here is the perfect place for the public stab in the back - not really the contradiction it may sound, since its whole success depends not so much in doing down a particular individual as in showing yourself up as the champion of a popular cause (popular, that is, in the eyes of *Them*, the authorities you aim to attract). The public backstab may be in one of the 'Synods' (national, diocesan, or ruri-decanal) with which the Church of England is now so plentifully provided. It may be in the press - the church press, since the national press is not likely to be interested; a book review can do it, or even a letter to the editor.

For use in all these cases there is a whole glossary of the humbly poisonous in language. Appropriate words include 'tendentious - prejudiced - unspiritual - modern'. Or alternatively, 'academic - specialist - intellectual' in order to damn with pseudo-praise. Frequent appearances in print or public, with a whole quiverful of such terms (to be used against suitable opponents, on behalf of the Establishment whose patronage one seeks), can be wonderfully effective in promoting you as 'reliable - solid - safe' - and in every way a good party hack and a trustworthy assassin. (But you must be careful with your use of language and ensure that your words cannot backfire. One Vicar, hoping for a discount on his garage bill, said 'I'm only a poor preacher.' 'I know,' retorted the mechanic, 'I've heard you.')

'GOING UP, GOING UP'

Doing others down is, for many, an agreeable exercise, like tearing off the wings of flies. But the elevation of self is, for others, the main purpose of the activity. How then should you - the ambitious Backstabber Clergyman - train yourself for the Clerical Success Handicap (apart from doping your rivals)? How do you make it to the top?

First of all, acquire a wife (unless you are going all out for saintly celibacy) as a permanent challenge to the spinsters of your parish. Some years ago, a writer to *The Times* suggested that for a clergyman to choose a wife for her 'suitability' was no better than for a clerk to pick the managing director's daughter for a spouse. What romantic nonsense! It is well known that at least one Bishop always marked his clergy's records with 'W.H.M.' (Wife Has Means) or 'W.I.' (Wife Impossible).

THE RIGHT WIFE FOR THE AMBITIOUS

In an ideal world, the perfect clergy wife has a title, as well as a suitable interest in the established Church. But sadly, the number of such ladies is small, so you may have to be content with hard cash or, at the very least, substantial expectations. Much better if the money is not earned income, since an employed wife will always cause some raised parochial eyebrows. But it is worth noting that under the curious system obtaining in the Church of England, any money earned by the clergy from extra work within the area of their ministry - chaplaincies, Easter offerings, wedding fees and such - is automatically deducted from their stipend. How much more prudent to breed pigs or write detective stories or encourage your wife to work - all of which will actually *add* to the family income.

Failing inherited money or earning capacity, your wife can usefully devote herself to 'good works' of a suitable sort. *Un*suitable good works include politics - even of a safely Conservative sort - the Arts, or anything which might be deemed 'putting herself forward'. This latter would include anything very striking in the way of clothes and appearance - although an ability to knock up a Cordon Bleu lunch when the Bishop has been taking Confirmation, or to produce superlative items for the cake stall at the parish sale, should never be disregarded.

'NOW BISHOP, IS THERE ANYTHING ELSE YOU FANCY?'

THE REV'D MRS

And here we cannot avoid reference to the ordination of women - although as the would-be successful clergyman you *must* make sure of the attitude of your Bishop before making any such allusion.

In this country, women can now be ordained Deacons, the first step towards the priesthood itself. This means that they can call themselves 'Reverend', wear clerical collars and conduct almost all the usual services except that of Holy Communion. However, if they happen to belong to parts of the Anglican Church outside the British Isles they can aspire to be Bishops, Archdeacons - the lot. This encourages us to anticipate the day when we are invited to meet 'The Right Reverend the Lady Bishop of Barchester', for whose sake the traditional episcopal apron and gaiters might well be resurrected in the form of a purple mini-skirt and matching stockings - although feminine Archdeacons may well prefer to drop their official title of 'The Venerable'!

In the light of these possibilities, we may hope that female Backstabbers will be amongst our readers. They may wonder whether, just as doctors so often marry doctors, they would be well advised to seek a clerical husband? I think the answer is 'No'. Parishes expect to get two for the price of one with clergy and their lay wives; they would be very hesitant about paying two salaries into one household for increased Revs!

PARSONAGE CHILDREN - DEMONS OR CHERUBS?

With a spouse, the Reverend Backstabber of either sex may, in time, produce children. This raises some very tricky problems. Many parishioners actually *like* to see youthful sin rampant in the vicarage, since it comforts them over the delinquency of their own offspring. Further, it provides very juicy bones of scandal to chew over the teacups or at the coffee morning. How cosy and consoling it then is to say 'I do feel so sorry for the dear Vicar and his wife. How heartbreaking for them when . . . ' Nevertheless, debauchery and drug-trafficking are not happy bedfellows in the episcopal palace and cathedral close (except in the eyes of the gutter press). Better, on the whole, to aim at producing choir-fodder and Sunday-school-teachers of a comfortably conformist type.

DOING YOUR OWN THING - BUT MAKE IT GOOD

Assuming that you have now acquired a suitable spouse and a couple of children (of an age and disposition to appear to great effect in the Christmas play in church), you can lift your eyes to the heights of promotion. As a Curate, you will have done your best to prove to the parishioners that the Vicar is a fuddy-duddy, and to the Vicar that you are ready for promotion - even at the cost of making yourself an intolerable nuisance. A word of warning here, should you be nearing the end of your Curacy and believe you might be in line for an important diocesan post: if your Vicar is cast in your own Backstabbing mould, and knows that your departure would immensely increase his own modest workload, he may - when asked by the Bishop for a reference - reply 'He's not quite ready for it yet, but in a year or two's time I've no doubt he'll do the job splendidly' (implication: 'I'm teaching him admirably, and it's really in his own interest that he shouldn't get the appointment just yet.'). You could find you stay firmly put in your present parish and never realise what befell you.

Now you have a parish of your own, or possibly a share in one of the increasingly popular 'team ministries'. It will not be enough just to do a good job of work: you must offer specialist expertise. Here your choice is largely dictated by your abilities. Are you, for instance, 'good with youth'? Can you run scouts, guides and all manner of clubs in such a way that the church hall does not become battle-scarred in a month and the cause of complaints about noise within a week? Can you actually persuade them all to appear in church and to avoid singing ribald versions of the hymns? However, guard against getting type-cast as a youth leader, otherwise you will remain *in situ* while your beard grows grey and your once-modern outlook starts to date.

Music is another useful expertise - though it is essential to remember you must never compete with the organist or choirmaster for the loyalty of the choir - any more than you should presume to suggest a change of hymn tune for any of the old faithfuls. The ability to rattle out popular favourites of fifty years ago at church socials is far more important than proficiency in Scarlatti.

Foreign missions, once a popular selling pitch, are now entirely *out* - as are all causes, however deserving, which could be termed 'political'! Support for the *status quo* is *not* considered 'political': right-wing parishes regard it as moral soundness, and left-wing ones believe the Church represents it in its purest form anyway. But that leaves plenty of ground for denunciation from the pulpit or in the parish magazine, and might actually lead to a quote in the national press - always good for the aspirant Backstabber image.

CHURCH POLITICS

Better by far to stick to church politics. And here the path, though complex to follow on the map, is fairly simple in practice. It begins at ground level with the church council, that body of 20 or 30 devout persons elected annually to 'co-operate with the incumbent in the work of the parish'. This means that *either* they sit placidly listening to, if not actually absorbing, accounts of what all the parish organisations have been up to of late; *or* they argue inconsequentially but ferociously over the cost of repairs to the bells, or the organ, or the gutters, or some part of church anatomy; *or* they make snide remarks as to why neighbouring congregations are so much larger than their own.

Next step up is the 'Diocesan Synod', with a bevy of committees fluttering round it. This can be an excellent way of catching the episcopal eye and ear, and attracting the attention of those lay persons who are influential in the diocese. It is essential, however, not to err in the direction of being amusing or exciting. Better - far better - to be seen as *sound* and *reliable*. In that way you will find yourself on one of those committees, hobnobbing with Archdeacons, High Sheriffs and retired colonels.

Play your cards carefully, and you may stand for election to the Nirvana of the 'Church Synod' itself, and spend days of every year trotting importantly in and out of Church House, Westminster, or gloating over gratifying extracts from your own speeches in *The Church Times*.

HIGH AND LOW - THE BACKSTABBER'S SEE-SAW

At this stage, if not before, it is advisable to declare ecclesiastical party allegiance. You can be 'High': addicted to the use of incense, elegant vestments in church and many-buttoned cassocks out of it; you insist on being called 'Father', and you are greatly attached to celebrating the feast days of obscure saints. Or you can be 'Low': once this meant puritan zeal; now it ranges from an insistence on 'Prayer Book Matins' (with absolutely nothing spared) to 'speaking with tongues', and gospel choruses accompanied on the guitar. These two attitudes - and their many subdivisions - form the two-party structure of the Church of England. There are, of course, in this as in the Parliament at Westminster a fringe group of mountebanks - and even a number of serious, intelligent and compassionate human beings - but you will not be interested in *them*.

For you have now - O Hallelujah! - caught the eye of that potent *eminence grise*, the Prime Minister's Ecclesiastical Secretary, and can dream of the day when the longed-for letter arrives from 10 Downing Street. But from this stage you wing your way into the celestial empyrean beyond *our* imaginings. Are you a Cathedral Dean, charged with raising £5,000,000 to keep your Cathedral upright on its foundations? An Archdeacon, captain of a team of clergymen who may well include emergent Backstabbers malevolently eyeing your prestige? A Diocesan or Suffragan Bishop? Or even - Hosanna, Hosanna! - an Archbishop? Are you, in short, Very Reverend, Venerable, Right Reverend, or indeed Most Reverend?

BACKSTABBING AT THE HIGHEST LEVELS

My own lack of high-level episcopal experience prevents me from offering inside information as to how their spiritual lordships operate at their Olympian heights - but one is tempted to enquire whether some amethyst-ringed hand might not be involved in the newspaper paragraphs which suggest likely nominees whenever a new Archbishop has to be found. To *name* an individual is to tip him the black spot. Backstabbers 'on the bench' are doubtless well aware of this, and likewise know how effective a word to the press from 'a reliable source' can be. The same technique was, of course, used most ingeniously by a former Press Secretary to the late Prime Minister in dealing with obstreperous Cabinet Ministers.

In silence we tiptoe from your presence, and can only conclude with a tombstone epitaph appropriate to all the Backstabbers we have met:

'This is going to hurt me much more than I have hurt you'

MEDICINE

by Lance Boyle

Even the caring profession has its share of Backstabbers - possibly more than most. Medical Backstabber is a cad, ruthlessly ambitious, dishonest, manipulative, amoral and selfish. At the same time he is charming, intelligent and brimming with charisma. While he is predominantly male, it would be foolish to neglect the number of highly successful female Backstabbers in the profession. Can it be you? Of course not - it is always easier to spot the Backstabber in others.

THE EMBRYONIC BACKSTABBER

It is not known exactly which specific genetic and environmental factors are necessary to create a Backstabber, but certain personality traits can be detected very early on in his life. Advances in medical science indicate that they may already be present when the fertilized ovum that is to become Backstabber implants itself in the wall of its mother's womb. Students of the genetic theory of character would argue that you are not to blame for your backstabbing behaviour. You were probably a tiresome baby, an insufferable infant and an impossible child. By the age of five you had mastered the art of manipulation. If a screaming tantrum did not get you what you wanted, you quickly learned to play one parent off against the other. Your home was where you first learned to divide and rule. It is a policy which will serve all Backstabbers well throughout their career.

Your background will preferably be solid middle-class professional - the breeding ground for the 'If you want it, go out and get it' Tory virtues. It does not help to be either too advantaged nor too disadvantaged: middle-of-the-road origins raise no eyebrows in the Medical Profession. Real Backstabbers know where they are going and will get there by whatever means.

MEDICAL SCHOOL

By a combination of cunning, intelligence, the bare minimum of hard work and a bit of subtle cheating, Backstabber will make sure of an interview for Medical School. To persuade the interview panel that you are their man (or woman), you must first dress with care. Go for the smart but casual look, avoiding any flamboyant bow ties (these are reserved for Consultants). Also avoid grey shoes and white socks - these are the kiss of death for any aspiring Backstabber.

Your first chance to undermine rivals presents itself in the waiting room, where you can use carefully crafted comments about their dress, exam results, athletic prowess, or any other detectable weaknesses. Make sure they know just how unpleasant the interviewers can be and what a grilling they can expect - they will all be quivering wrecks by the time their names are called. By contrast, you will be confident and alert: you swiftly convince the panel of your ability, your dedication and your wide range of interests in both science and the arts. Remarkably they all fall for it and accept you.

At Pre-clinical School, Backstabber excels at being in the right place at the right time. Lectures are tedious and crowded - it is not easy for you to stand out and gain advantage. But equally, no-one notices if you are not there. In true backstabbing tradition, you do not waste your energies on lectures. Instead you cultivate the friendship of keener female colleagues who take meticulous notes in legible handwriting - then you photocopy the important bits you need.

Unlike lectures, tutorials cannot be avoided. Not that self-promoting Backstabber would want to anyway. Not for you a quiet seat in the back row out of the tutor's sight. You will show keen interest and gain the upper hand by raising questions only on those subjects about which you are well informed (otherwise your tutor may question you on subjects about which you are so totally ignorant that you cannot even pronounce their names).

Practical classes will afford Backstabber perfect opportunities to sabotage other students' efforts. Such ploys as an accidental nudge of the microscope in histology, losing the vital field so that your rivals have no hope of seeing what they are meant to see, or the adulteration of some vital ingredient in biochemistry or pharmacology practicals, are par for the course for you. Backstabber finds anatomy dissection distasteful and naturally leaves colleagues to do most of the donkey work. Once they have painstakingly laid bare, say, the nervous system of a hand, you raise yours and call a demonstrator with a pertinent question. All your fellow-students will be elbowed brusquely out of the way as you and the demonstrator pore over the arm. You will get the credit for having done all the difficult work, and the demonstrator will think you are a splendid chap for allowing him to show off his expertise on the median, ulnar and radial nerves in front of the students. At exam time, you can ensure your success by performing your own 'medical cuts' and appropriating as many essential textbooks as possible from the Medical School library. Your rivals will spend so long hunting for the missing books that they will have no time to revise.

BLADEWORK ON THE WARD

Once you have passed your pre-clinical exams, you will need to hone your skills for the teaching ward rounds. As a student, you will be assigned patients who are under the care of a Consultant. Backstabber knows that it is important to be seen and heard on the Consultant's round, as long as you make sense. To look foolish would be a disaster. Impressing the Consultant means good grades and a possible house job on qualifying. When you are stuck for a diagnosis, always call it a virus. And when you are completely baffled, diagnose an allergy.

Keeping in with the houseman will enable you to excel on ward rounds. Familiarise yourself with the full medical history of any patients to be seen on the teaching round and help the houseman with all the troublesome chores, such as taking blood samples. Visit the patients you have been allocated every day, and encourage them to impress upon the Consultant what a wonderful young doctor they have. That's you of course. Scupper your rivals by hiding their notes and X-rays: the Consultant will be infuriated and your colleagues left wearing a look of mystified incompetence.

Always be in the operating theatre during a Consultant's list. Make sure that you are the one who is pulling on the retractor during a long abdominal operation. Entertain the surgeon and anaesthetist with your lively banter, while the rest of the students desperately try to look interested from their position of poor visibility behind your left shoulder. The Consultant will fire questions at these shuffling layabouts, and as part of the surgical team you can join in the subdued chortles when the student gets it wrong. To complete your acceptance in the surgical camaraderie, it is vital to chat up the scrub-sister. You have already decided that of all the specialities, surgery is the one most suited to your temperament - it will be your route to the top, with the scrub-sister as your ally.

EXTRA-CURRICULAR INTERESTS

Ambition is meat and drink to Backstabber. You will have no time left for any other interests. You will not be found puking with the lads after the rugger club dinner, or in hot pursuit of any stunning new nurse or lissom physiotherapist at the sweaty student disco. You never get involved in the festive fun of handing out Christmas presents in the wards dressed up as Santa Claus or one of his reindeer: it would never be forgotten if you were the one who killed the patient with a weak heart because he thought he was being resuscitated by Rudolf. Equally, you are unlikely to be an ardent fell-walker, thespian or ornithologist. However, knowing that image is everything, you will take up other interests whenever you can see an advantage in it. For instance, if the Professor of Surgery is president of the sailing club, you join up faster than you can raise a spinnaker. The roughest sea crossing will never put you off crewing on the Professor's yacht.

Backstabber is not a romantic. You are not particularly interested in love, nor do you have any instinct for sex - that is merely another diversion to get in the way of your final goal. Instead, employ your considerable charm for a purpose, such as acquiring others' lecture notes or inside knowledge of exams. Since you are now well in with the professorial surgical unit, you will have noticed the needs of the rather plain, over-worked and underloved Miss Cutter, the surgical Senior Registrar in her late thirties. Chat her up at the bar, make her feel interesting and desirable: take her to the opera, and to expensive restaurants she has never had time to find out about before, let alone eat at; and then have quiet evenings at home sipping Veuve Cliquot, listening to Puccini and eating exquisite suppers you cook yourself. You are talented, you have learned your lessons well - Miss Cutter is overwhelmed. She embarks on a torrid love affair the like of which she has only ever read about in books. She helps you with your revision for your finals, and you spend your evenings lying naked in front of a fire as you practise a clinical examination of Miss Cutter filmed on a borrowed video. Even Backstabber finds this perversely erotic.

Miss Cutter will now make sure that you are in line for appointment as House Surgeon. She will even provide you with a list of the patients attending the Royal College of Surgeons for the clinical exams. With this sort of help you will not only get a pass with distinction in surgery, but you will also win the Gold Medal and be appointed House Surgeon to the professorial unit. Miss Cutter believes she has made sure her lover will remain with her for a bit longer, and dreams wistfully of marriage and children. But this is certainly not yet in your scheme of things.

HOUSE JOBS

House jobs are murder, even for Backstabber. The hours are long and antisocial, sleep is interrupted by constant bleeping, there is an endless round of clerking new patients, pre-op preparation, operating lists, ward rounds, ensuring that all the X-rays and blood test results are up to date and on hand, and being 'on-take' for emergency admissions. The dedicated doctor takes this in his stride, the mediocre muddle along, and a few collapse under the strain. Backstabber will use all his wiles and guile to ensure that life is made as easy as possible in the circumstances. Miss Cutter will be less useful now, and anyway there are more important contacts to nurture.

A houseman's life can be made a misery by any number of people. First, there is the Night Sister who bleeps him out of his bed. Then there is the bleep operator herself, the social worker who cannot find placements for troublesome patients, the receptionist in X-ray who cannot possibly fit another patient onto her crowded lists for at least another two days, or the pathology secretary who sends up the wrong test results. But within weeks of starting, the Backstabber houseman has the situation under control. A box of chocolates here, a bunch of flowers there, dinner with the X-ray receptionist, and even a bonk with the social worker or the night sister whenever they are feeling miserable. It works a treat. They all adore you and will do anything for you. The night sister will bleep another houseman, there is never any delay in getting X-rays done, and the social worker miraculously clears beds the Consultant thought would be blocked for weeks. You are a great success. There is no chance of these relationships turning sour: house jobs only last for six months.

WARD ROUNDS

On ward rounds, Backstabber appears slick and efficient. Your patient notes are always updated and tests carried out. Without exception your rivals are always less efficient. This is easy to arrange: it's not difficult to lose a batch of blood test results. The obliging bleep operator will arrange for your rival to be called away just before the Consultant's ward round commences. Similarly you can use her to extract you from tricky situations. Your rivals will be in a permanent state of despair. They do not have the ear of the X-ray receptionist or the pathology secretary (let alone any other part of their body). Your presentations are clear and concise, while those of your rivals are flustered and confused. Backstabber uses the system: everyone else blames it.

When it comes to responsibilities, Backstabber will always

volunteer to take on more than his full share. You relish the chance to organise the housemans' on-call rota, as this means you will be able to avoid duties at Christmas, Easter and Bank Holidays or the two extra NHS Holidays - St COHSE Day and St NUPE Day. You willingly offer to act as the chairman of the Doctors' Mess, where you collect subscriptions, rake off a bit for your trouble, and earn a little bit more by careful negotiation with suppliers. You gain credit for running it well and for organising excellent parties and dinners, where you ply influential Consultants with booze and act the perfect host. You bully your assistants into organising a raffle to raise money for the special care baby unit. The first prize is a week's fishing on the Spey: you nobble the draw and win it, then made a great issue of saying you cannot possibly accept it and offer it instead to your Consultant. He will have no hesitation whatsoever in accepting it. Thereafter, the merest mention of your name will bring the Consultant out in a warm flush of contented affection.

EXTRA CASH

This is always welcome, and it is one of the profession's rewards for the avid Backstabber. By successfully ingratiating yourself with your Consultant it will be you - not any of your rival colleagues - who is invited to assist in his private operations (for private read lucrative). You get the afternoon off, pulling on your old friend the retractor and - blissfully! - getting paid for it.

Another great source of income is signing cremation forms (the doctor receives a fee every time he signs one). Sleeping with the night sister is still paying dividends - she will bleep you first thing in the morning to let you know of any deaths on the ward. You hot-foot it down to the basement to see the mortuary attendant. He has a monopoly on the dead and is wealthy beyond belief. He is said to own a castle in Scotland, for there is a fortune to be made in the death business. Sign as many 'crem' forms as possible. There will still be plenty of money left over after you have given the mortuary attendant his occasional cut, plus a couple of cases of Glenfiddle-it. When rival doctors complain, the mortuary attendant merely says that he tried bleeping them but couldn't get a reply. No-one will take the complaint any further: non-Backstabbers feel it is indecent to take money from the dead anyway.

THE CAREER LADDER

As a Backstabber, you will continue to use the same tactics as you move up the career ladder - from houseman to senior house officer, registrar and senior registrar. You will get the prestigious posts with influential bosses. Your *curriculum vitae* is immaculate and your interview technique perfect. You know that you can perform well; you concentrate on getting the other candidates rattled. You recognise that interviews are a courtship ritual, not a battle for survival, and as such you will thoroughly enjoy them. In the waiting room, hand round the tea or coffee (liberally spiked with a benzodiazepine tranquilliser) to the other candidates, or offer them some chocolate (do not mention it is Ex-lax). That should get them going. At one interview (for a post he didn't want), one Backstabber deliberately destroyed his own chances: 'Are you married?' he was asked. He replied 'I am not.' 'Do you have a girlfriend?' 'No.' 'Are you by any chance a homosexual?' was the next question. 'No,' replied the Backstabber, 'Do I have to be to work here?'

As a junior doctor you will find that appearing busy is the best way of avoiding hard work. If your Consultant catches you drinking coffee during Out-patients Clinic he is sure to off-load the rest of his list onto you. Always keep a large pile of patient notes at hand: in the Clinic, everyone will assume you still have lots of patients to see; in the corridor, they will assume that you are rushing off to see other patients; in reality, you are off for a quick kip.

PATIENTS ON THE WARD

Unfortunately, at this stage in your career you still have to deal directly with patients (later on they can be forgotten entirely and you can concentrate on numbers and money). But as a Backstabber you will have developed a system for removing difficult patients. It is called transferring them. Complicated patients usually have more than one thing wrong with them and can therefore be booted out into other specialities. If they have loose bowels or no movement at all - send them to Gastroenterology (where one sparky patient, tired of being quizzed daily by Sister about the regularity of his movements, concealed an ornament under his bedclothes - a fully-rigged sailing ship inside an antique glass bottle. When Sister appeared next morning he produced it with a flourish, saying 'Here you are, Sister - a ship I passed in the night.') If they are over 60, send them to Geriatrics. If they complain too much, shout, roll their eyes, or ask for second helpings at meal-times, the Psychiatrists will have them. A bit of a chest pain - Cardiology. Where there is no obvious chance of referral, you will have to engineer it. Catching the urinary catheter in the lift door is a good method. You will become an expert at disposing of difficult patients, while gaining much credit for emptying your beds and saving money on the ward.

You must be equally adept at poaching interesting or lucrative patients and stealing diagnoses. If you hear that some influential person has been admitted to Cardiology, be at his bedside in a flash. Convince both patient and staff that it is essential to operate on the man's hernia immediately: you will get all the credit for the patient's recovery under your care and gain vital contacts in the halls of power.

GETTING AHEAD

In the Operating Theatre it is important to achieve supremacy over the other junior surgeons. Make sure that the dyslexic scrub-nurse is always assigned to your rivals. She will invariably miscount the swabs at the end of the procedure and the surgeon will have to delve around inside the abdomen for the lost swabs in a panic before the count is rectified. Or you can slip a pair of artery forceps behind the patient's back when an X-ray is taken during surgery. They will appear to have been left in the abdomen, and when your rival operates to recover them it won't just be the patient who is stitched up.

To get ahead it is essential to have accomplished some successful research. The output of research is measured in terms of the number of publications in the medical scientific literature,

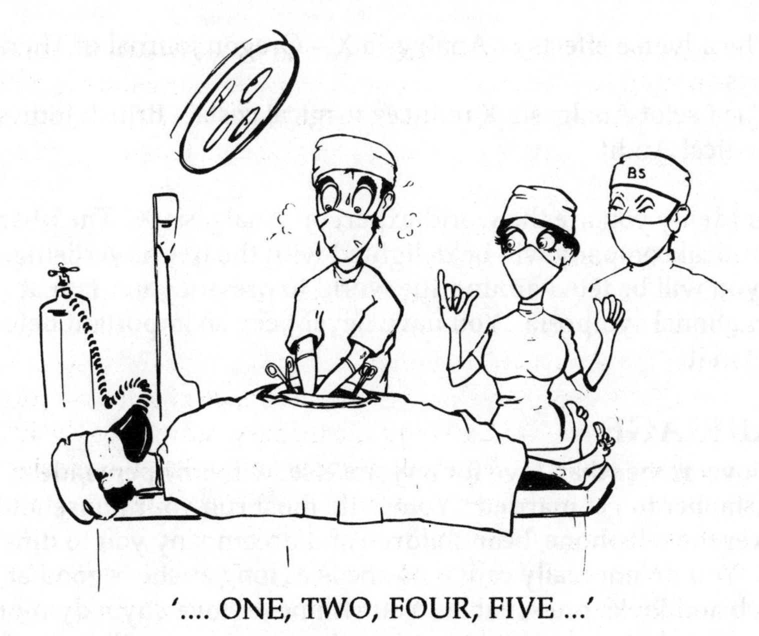

'.... ONE, TWO, FOUR, FIVE ...'

rather than their benefit to mankind. The name of the game is 'Publish or Perish'. Backstabber is always on the hunt for more publications. The best way is to encourage doctors in full-time research to carry out work on your patients: for research doctors to gain critical credibility they will have to include you as a joint author every time. It's a cinch.

The simplest way to boost your publication list is duplication. If you take the trouble to do the work at all, make sure that you squeeze as much academic mileage out of it as possible. Write up the same piece of work from several different angles, under different titles for different journals. For example, if you are paid by a pharmaceutical company to trial a new post-operative pain-killer, don't publish the study as a single work. Your final publication list should read:

'Analgesia X reduces pain following partial gastrectomy' - Scandinavian Journal of Abdominal Surgery

'Reduction in acute psychoses following Analgesia X usage' - Archives of Psychiatry

'The adverse effects of Analgesia X' - Oregon Journal of Therapeutics

'The use of Analgesia X reduces surgical costs' - British Journal of Medical Audit

Suddenly you are the world expert on Analgesia X. The pharmaceutical company will be delighted with the free advertising, and you will be fêted around the world to present your data at international symposia. You have never been so important before. Revel in it.

MARRIAGE

Self-love, rather than love for anyone else, will now persuade Backstabber to get married. Your wife must run your household, answer the telephone, bear children and accompany you to dinners. You do not really care who she is as long as she is good at the job and looks presentable. You will never love anybody more than yourself, but you will be rich and your partner will do well financially in what you regard as a purely commercial union. Over the years you will have collected social contacts like other people collect antiques: you should easily be able to find a peer's daughter or an heiress. Failing this, you could always marry into the business - a nurse, a physiotherapist or even another doctor. Whoever she is, her ambition must be limited to making sure it is you rather than she who succeeds.

THE CONSULTANT

When you become a fully accredited Specialist, you may have to wait until the right consultancy post comes your way. Once you have a signed contract with the National Health Service you can make your juniors really sweat for their living, while you get your own private practice under way. The NHS salary is useful to tide you over, but the real money comes from the operating lists at private hospitals. Tempting though it may seem, you will avoid blatant advertising - but you will still make sure the word gets round that you are the best man to send private patients to. The success of private practice depends on the three A's: availability, affability and ability. In that order. For a fee, you will be happy to see a patient at any time. For an extra fee, you will be friendly. For a ludicrous fee, you will even give them a diagnosis.

CUTTING THE WAITING LISTS

Back in the NHS hospital, the successful Backstabber will tackle some of the grass-root problems. As a newly-appointed Consultant you will have inherited a long waiting list for elective surgery. Get your secretary to go through the list: some patients will have died, others will have left the area or run out of patience and been treated privately. Following your established practice, any difficult patients will be immediately transferred elsewhere, thereby increasing the patient load of your rival colleagues. At a stroke, you will have cut the list by a half. Shorten it still further by making your juniors work longer hours. Overloading your juniors and colleagues is a management strategy from which Backstabber will reap immense rewards: you will be acknowledged by health ministerial officials as their type of person, the thoroughly modern NHS Consultant Manager.

SLASH AND BURN - THE NEW MANAGEMENT STYLE

Backstabber Consultant will be the ideal manager. You will chair committees ruthlessly. Decisions are no longer made by consensus: the loudest and most bullish voice wins the day - make sure that it's yours. Money follows the patient in the new NHS, and as far as you are concerned it can follow anyone it wants as long as it eventually finishes up in your pocket. Your research account will increase steadily, topped up by pharmaceutical companies on a regular basis for services which are often unclear but which finance your trips abroad to present research carried out by your juniors.

Audit is the flavour of the month for today's Backstabber - 'efficient use of resources' is the catch-phrase. Your colleagues may be slow on the up-take, but to you 'audit' means creative accounting - something at which you are a natural. Figures will show that you have the fastest patient turnover, the shortest waiting lists and the lowest post-operative infection rate. Your colleagues will be at a loss to know how you do it. Your success is recognised, you get a substantial rise in income in the form of merit awards, and take three steps closer to your knighthood.

THE FALL

During the cut and thrust of your career you will have made a number of enemies, and you will need to keep your wits about you if you are to avoid coming a cropper. For a few Backstabbers the strain becomes too much: a life-time of intrigue and blade-work has taken its toll. Their wives have long since left them, and their children have run wild and turned to drink and drugs. Some Backstabbers become alcoholics, others become addicted to controlled substances. Their careers nosedive. Other Backstabbers just go dotty - they start by losing control of their direction, then end up with a permanent residency in a padded cell. Others still never actually lose their senses, they merely beat the system once too often and at last get their just deserts. Caught out for fraud, negligence, unprofessional behaviour or scandal, they are forced into ignominy and early retirement.

THE PINNACLE

Top Backstabbers will avoid these pitfalls. For them they sky's the limit. Some strive for an academic chair, but the wiliest know that the life of a British university professor is an uphill struggle against plummeting budgets and the brain drain. The pinnacle of your career will be achieved by your skill in economics, not Medicine. You will be in the New Year's Honours List not so much for medical achievement as for doing the the dirty on your colleagues and saving money - your 'K' would more accurately stand for 'Knifehood'.

The newly-knighted Backstabber will acquire an interest in shooting and fishing: this will suit your image and help maintain contacts. You will have a second house in the south of France, and spend your holidays in the French Alps or the Caribbean with your second - or probably third - wife. Your children, if you have not lost contact with them altogether, will visit you periodically to present the grandchildren (usually as an excuse to ask for money).

THE OBITUARY

Backstabbers usually live to a great age. You will refuse to give your enemies the satisfaction of dying. You will remain difficult and cantankerous until the end by making controversial statements to the press. When your Maker can no longer find an excuse for further delay, you will make your final journey. In due course, your name will appear - for the last time! - in the most popular section of the British Medical Journal - the Obituaries. Certain phrases will only thinly disguise the Backstabber character:

'A forceful character' (He always got his own way)

'A man not afraid to speak his mind' (He was blunt and abusive)

'A gilded career' (He lined his pockets well)

'He remained too busy to enjoy his retirement' (He remained an interfering old buffer to the end)

'A demanding colleague' (All his juniors suffered nervous breakdowns)

And if you are at all puzzled by the letters 'RIP' which appear at the end of the obit, remember they also stand for 'Rot In Perpetuity'.

THE ARMY

by Ivor Future

A staff car returning a General from a Regimental Dinner late one evening, broke down in the middle of the countryside. The General's driver - a shapely female soldier - apologised, alighted and, tool-kit in hand, opened the bonnet. A few minutes later the General emerged to see how she was getting on. 'Want a screwdriver?' he asked helpfully. 'Might as well, Sir,' she replied, 'The car's had it.'

To find out how to qualify for such perks (and many more besides) as a very senior officer in the British Army, read on. For the younger officer, this guide will set you on the right path to those coveted gold and red collar tabs, slinky black staff car with slinky-backed female driver, fatboys' lunches, the eventual directorship in the City and a cottage in Wiltshire. For the old and successful, it will reassure you that you got it right. For those who did not make it, it will tell you how the bastards knifed you while your back was turned.

SETTING THE SCENE

What did you see in the shaving mirror this morning? A steely-eyed, khaki killer with a well-chiselled jawline and dazzling smile, whose lithe, athletic posture spelt - intelligence, AMBITION, energy, AMBITION, razor-sharp mind, AMBITION, resourcefulness, AMBITION, and AMBITION! 'We've got it, Mister,' you said to your image, 'We are going to the top and don't care who we have to tread on to get there!' Admit it now, you are an out-

and-out military S. H. one T. - a Backstabber - outrageously ambitious, with the morals of an alley cat, whose rationale is that the end justifies the means. You are thoroughly unscrupulous, and covertly mean, dishonest and vindictive when required. You recognise that there are no mere players - only winners and losers and 'If you want to play poker with your career that's fine by me, but I'm going to play with a stacked deck.' In military parlance, 'There is no limit to exploitation' - and your mission is to get to the pinnacle of the Army by any means possible.

If you empathise with this level of motivation, then you are the man for me, and a luxurious red leather armchair on the Army Board is undoubtedly waiting for you. There are only two kinds of animal in the gladiatorial arena of a military career - the Backstabber and the Victim - and you must learn to recognise both types from the start.

THE BACKSTABBER

An officer but no gentleman. Although ambitious in the extreme, he will never admit to it in public. Has an air of being permanently cool, calm and collected. Is always in the know, knows what's what, who's who, and who is doing what to whom. Joined the Army from one of the 'recognised' public schools, followed by Oxbridge or Durham. Has an innate sense of his own worth, but knows that, because he is not quite up to scratch, he has got to mark his card. Come what may, he is going to be Chief of Staff (COS) of a Brigade, command his Battalion of The Royal Regiment of Foot in Mouth (Queen Anthrax's Own MCVXVIIIth of Foot), and command an Armoured Brigade and Division *en route* to any position on the Army Board. Knows that the soldiers follow him because he will screw them if they don't, and that success in the Army goes to those who are ruthless enough to climb over the bodies of Victims who get in the way.

THE VICTIM

The epitome of an officer and a gentleman. An idealistic, innocent and thoroughly nice chap in the 1st Battalion The Good Guys. Joined the Army straight from an ordinary public - or even grammar - school, having been brought up on a diet of VC stories from the front page of *Victor* and tales of how his grandfather survived trench foot in the glorious dugouts of the Somme. (Also believes that all policemen are straight, and that no-one in the City would stoop to insider dealing.) Is reasonably clever, industrious, terribly enthusiastic about his job, and genuinely cares about the 'boys'. Believes the soldiers follow him because he is a natural leader (and not just out of curiosity), and that the Army is a meritocracy where the top positions are filled by the best officers.

KNOWING WHO'S WHO AND WHAT'S WHAT

An intimate knowledge of who is commanding what, where and how well, is an essential part of refined military backstabbing. Your reputation within the Regiment as the 'man in the know', and the chance to plot your own future postings, will depend upon such intelligence. Similarly, you should also be aware of 'what's what' in any topical conversation at the General's dining table. This will enable you to converse on equal terms with both the Commanding Officer and the Brigadier, both of whom (once they have noticed that you have friends in high places) will frequently seek your informed opinion.

As a career Backstabber officer, you must have a sound knowledge of the constituent elements of the Army, and be able to recognise their archetypal officers at a glance - especially the senior ones. This ability will be invaluable: whenever you enter a room you will know immediately with whom you should be seen talking. Furthermore, it will save you the embarrassment of discovering that the Brigadier you have spent the last two hours buttering up is only Director of the Catering Corps, while the Colonel you cut dead is the future Divisional Commander.

Basically, there are only four types of officer in the British Army:

THE CAVALRY OFFICER

THE GAY YOUNG BLADE

He will be thin, with a gaunt face, patrician nose and raucous laugh. His dress sense is a deliberate attempt at stylish nonchalance, which fails due to the absence of Nanny's helping hand. On the whole, he will regard the Army as the best hobby he ever took up, and the cheapest way of maintaining the standard of living to which his family has been accustomed for generations. He sees himself as the 'gay young blade' of the Army. Let him continue to think so.

THE INFANTRY OFFICER

Infantry officers vary as much as their many regiments in history, colour, character, religious beliefs and sexual proclivities. He will be an affable chap, with a ruddy complexion born of too many days on mountain tops and open heathland. He is not very intelligent, and joined the family or county Regiment for want of something better to do in his early 20's. Conservative in his dress, he likes huntin', shootin' and fishin', and has a strange predilection for ditches and trenches. In every Regiment, there will always be one 'gadget man' - a walking advertisement for every conceivable snazzy gadget for the 'combat environment'. He will sport everything from Gortex Y-fronts to a handy device for making gloves out of live rabbits (the Marigold Combat Coney Liner).

GADGET MAN

THE TECHNOCRAT

The technical intelligentsia of the Army are to be found in the Gunners, the Engineers (Construction, Electrical and Mechanical), and the Signals. He is the *arriviste* of the Army, and is currently on the up and up due to the technological explosion. Frightfully keen and totally unintelligible, he will be easy to identify by his flat cap, whippet, hybrid accent and technical manual. He joined the Army for the technical challenge. Let him have it - the power *you* are after is not to be found in 3-pin plugs.

THE TECHNOCRAT

THE REST

There is a veritable multitude of other officers in 'the rest' of the Army, comprised of cooks, bottle-washers, blanket-stackers, policemen and sundry other menials, all needed to help oil the cogs of the military machine. Any one of them is instantly recognisable by his worn, hangdog expression, balding pate and sagging jowl (and he is only a Subaltern). His dress sense is appalling. He is the 'train spotter' of the military world, complete with anorak and duffle bag, and joined the Army because it was the only organisation that would have him. He poses no threat to Backstabber, and may safely be ignored.

THE REST

ONE-UPMANSHIP

When in the company of other officers (your rivals) you must practise Regimental One-Upmanship. You must always drop the nick-names of senior officers of your acquaintance, and ensure that your wife makes frequent reference not only to 'Our time at Staff College' but also to your '*Outstanding*' annual reports and likelihood of early promotion. Modesty is *not* the name of Backstabber's game. Nevertheless you should have sufficient subtlety to refrain from telling a Frenchman that there are trees down the Champs Elysees only because the Germans like marching in the shade. When you invite other officers to dinner, display your Staff College photograph prominently, hang the personally dedicated picture of yourself and the (Royal) Colonel in Chief above the loo, and leave the leather-bound copy of your British Army Review Paper lying carelessly on the coffee table - almost concealed by the *Tatler*. They will get the message.

COMMAND - Seize command whenever you can - don't wait for it to be handed to you. Never forget that some are born great and some achieve greatness, but bloody few actually have it thrust upon them.

OPINIONS - Have them in abundance and expound your views at every opportunity. The only other opinion that counts is that of your boss (unless, of course, his own boss is present, in which case you both agree with the senior officer). Your survival depends upon your ability to judge the nuances in any situation, and you must be all things to all men (a chameleon with teeth!).

MEMOS AND LETTERS TO YOUR BOSS - Send your boss an occasional memo or silent copy of a letter, to show him how clever you have been. If possible, inform him how you have already rectified a problem that your chosen Victim had not foreseen (because you never warned him).

BRIEFS AND MINUTES OF MEETINGS - Produce briefs regularly for your boss so that he is made aware of how much effort you are putting into your job. The details are immaterial because he will not have time to read them all fully, but he will thank you profusely nonetheless. When Secretary of a meeting, ensure you appropriate the most rewarding actions for yourself (as Secretary, you can omit to minute the more onerous ones - everyone will have forgotten the details by the next meeting).

COMPLEX MATTERS - Do not touch them. There are far too many Pooh traps and hidden obstacles to trip you up. Palm them off on a Victim, saying they are 'Much too complicated for a guns-and-trenches chap like me to understand'. He will be too busy sorting them out to ever see the easy points you are scoring.

IMMEDIATE DECISIONS - To be avoided at all costs. Whenever possible, divert these thorny problems to a Victim. But if all else fails - procrastinate.

SOLVING FUTURE PROBLEMS - If you keep your ear to the ground at Regimental coffee, in the Mess, or on the tube to Waterloo you should glean some good ideas. Use these to gain a reputation as a conceptual thinker, adept at solving problems before they become apparent to the powers that be. If you hear a really cracking idea, grab it, modify it, adapt it *and brief it as your own.*

BADGE AND GONG-COLLECTING - Find time to start the jolly game of badge-collecting, so as to appear amazingly well trained (they will also look superb in the portrait of you in your Blues which will eventually hang in the Regimental Mess). Parachute wings are essential for tactical credibility. A sub-division of this game is gong-collecting: you should collect as many as possible (ensuring that you are never shot at, bombed or kidnapped by Shi-ites). Some medals come free with your cornflakes - plus doing 27 shifts as Watchkeeper in Northern Ireland, or for water ski-ing while killing time as a member of the UN in Cyprus.

ROCKING THE BOAT - Don't! Progressive radicals are barely tolerated as Subalterns. The higher you climb, the more dangerous it becomes to inject new ideas into the monolith. To try and change this will probably cost you your career. Haven't you noticed that Generals only resign on a point of principle once they have realised they are not going any further?

TREATMENT OF SUBORDINATES - To gain the undivided loyalty of your juniors, make sure you give them a good kicking early on in their tour with you. Ideally this should be done while they are in their sleeping bags on exercise and have consumed several beers - enabling you to deny all knowledge of the incident in the morning. If they get uppity, repeat the treatment every night until they understand who is boss.

SOME USEFUL TERMS

The brighter readers of this *Guide* will have realised that there is a plethora of abbreviations and military jargon with which you must be familiar if you are to have any chance of making conversation - let alone a career - within the Army. To help you get it right, here is a short glossary of the most essential terms:

Army Board: Collection of dead wood that creaks under pressure

BAOR: British Army Of the Rhine: 55,000 soldiers wondering what they are doing and if they will be home for Christmas

Backstabber: The chap you saw in the mirror this morning

Cavalry Officers: Odd assortment of aristocratic eccentrics too idle to work in the City

DOE: Department of Excuses (responsible for military housing)

4-Star General: High-powered essence that drives the Army. Can be highly volatile if not handled properly

Gunners: Inexplicably, the butt of Army humour

Infantry: The stage between childhood and adultery

Masonic Handshake: Normal greeting between members of the Army Board

1 BR Corps: From the French, meaning a cold dead body

RMAS: Royal Military Academy Sandhurst - the officers' prep school, steeped in history, tradition and more than a little bullshit

Regiment: A medium-sized Army formation, referred to with the prefix 'The ...'. Joined by career officers

Subaltern: An officer of low rank, negligible influence, no morals and negative bank balance

Thruster: Generic term for an ambitious career officer (but not necessarily a Backstabber)

WRAC: Women's Royal Army Corps (also Warm Round And Cuddly)

OTHER HELPFUL HINTS

FAMILY TIES

Two types of family are important to the military Backstabber: ancient and modern. 'Ancient' family means your own and your wife's relations, and there is not a lot you can do about any of these. If your family let you down by allowing you to develop a regional accent, you must eradicate it. Perfect an 'Okay, yah' Sloane Ranger drawl before you get to Sandhurst. You may have to acquire something with a more Gaelic flavour if you get accepted into a Scottish Regiment: the odd 'I'm awa the noo for a wee dram wi' ma bonnies' may reassure your new Commanding Officer that you are a jolly good chap. Similarly, in 'proper' Regiments, officers have good 'U' names (Charles, William and Edward) thoughtfully bestowed at birth by forward-thinking parents. As youngsters they are known as (a proper) Charlie, Willy and Neddy (or Donkey - as in 'big ears', rather than 'hung like a . . '). As you grow older and more astute, revert to the least scatological derivation of your forenames.

'Modern' family is a mistake of your own making! You should enjoy a long and successful bachelorhood - sowing wild oats hither and thither, whilst praying for crop failure.

MARRIAGE TIES

Before getting hitched, you must pay heed to the *Incontrovertible Army Law of Marriage (Officers)*: Subaltern (never), Captain (may), Major (should), and Colonel (must). This law is broken at your peril. You should find and marry your firm young filly only *after* you have enlightened her about her supporting role to the main feature. Ideally, marry a General's daughter: she will have seen it all before, she will not need any training on regimental vagaries and Mess decorum, and Mummy will have told her how to take a lover discreetly while you are immersed in your career. As a bonus, Daddy will see that your career blossoms for her sake, and his chums will be wary of doing down the son-in-law of an Army Board member.

OLD SCHOOL TIES

You should have a number of Old School connections with the Regiment in particular, and the Army in general. While you are still at Sandhurst, volunteer to help run your old school's Combined Cadet Force: this will bring you to the attention of the 'Old Boy' Generals, who are invited to come and inspect it at regular intervals. (Furthermore, if you are still servicing the housemaster's daughter, the Army will obligingly pay your travelling expenses.) This will almost certainly guarantee you an easy ride through to Commissioning, and perhaps a College prize to boot - especially if the College Commander is himself an Old Boy.

SOCIAL TIES

This is your wife's province, but you will be responsible for pointing her antennae towards the prime sources of gossip and information. She must never miss a Regimental Coffee Morning, Ladies' Dinner Night or Tupperware Party, otherwise you will become the topic of conversation and referred to as someone who 'ought to be bloody well hung'. (*You* should never miss an Ann Summers Evening - you might become the subject of conversation on who *is* bloody well hung!) When dealing with the wives of senior officers, give them the deference they consider to be consistent with their husband's position: his rank + 2.

DRESS

There are very few rules governing dress in the Army, but those that do exist are firmly adhered to. The general rule of thumb is: 'In uniform, no two officers should ever dress identically - even if members of the same Regiment or Corps. Out of uniform, the reverse applies.' Acceptable civilian clothes are smart but casual: a combination of cords, Viyella checked shirt, Guernsey sweater and highly-polished brown brogues. Of course, Backstabber will leave nothing to chance and you will insist on buying all your own clothes - only Victims allow their wives to shop in M&S on their behalf. Above all, never wear anything that makes you look like a 'squaddie'.

RELIGION

Backstabber will regularly volunteer to organise the Regimental Church Parade (although naturally your Subalterns will do all the work while you play Chief Pharisee). You must ascertain in advance the religion of both the Regimental and Brigade Commanders and be prepared, if necessary, to convert. But beware of pitfalls: Anglicans are always very sedate in Church, and wear dark suits and regimental ties; Roman Catholics smile and sing folk songs, have up to five children in tow and wear sweaters and cords; Methodists like a good dose of fire and brimstone and wear frowns. A senior Army officer of any other religious persuasion does not exist.

POLITICS

Unless you are seriously rich (or politics are beneath you because of your seat in the Upper House), you will be true blue Tory. If you belong to the Vulgar Fractional Cavalry you may be fashionably pink Liberal, but will veer away from anything too radical as unproven, and therefore suspect. The Corps have Labour tendencies and must always be watched as possible subversives.

SEX

In some Regiments it is believed to be compulsory, but not in the Household Division, who have horses, dogs and jolly girlfriends in Chelsea as substitutes. Shirt-lifting is allowable as it was common practice at public school, but bonking soldiers is definitely frowned upon - even if you restrict yourself to female ones. Nurses, teachers and Norland Nannies are fair game, but do not let them deflect you from the real prize: a suitable woman to support you in your climb to the top. After marriage you should only need to complete the connubial function twice - unless you get twins first time.

ANIMALS

Dogs are scaled and issued at Sandhurst. Officers' dogs should be given original yet amusing names like 'Effindog' (as in 'Come here, you effin' dog'). Or like the famous Brigadier who had three whippets called 'Whippetin', 'Whippetout' and 'Wipeit'. NB: Career officers do not own cats.

FITNESS

As a young officer you need only be fit enough to fornicate. As a mid-ranking officer you should still look that fit, but it is unlikely that it will be officially put to the test. A Colonel needs only to be fit for promotion, and a General probably needs only to be fit for retirement. Physical exercise does not enter into it.

MONEY

Old family money is preferable, although new money is acceptable if it comes in wheelbarrow-loads. Failing ownership or inheritance of a family fortune, you should marry it. Either way, try and have some of your own as the Government will give you precious little of theirs.

ALCOHOL

Backstabber will not drink in public since it inhibits the sensory perception and limits your consciousness of which senior officer was present when such-and-such was said about so-and-so to whom, and who was listening at the time. This does not mean that you cannot drink at all, but only allow yourself to get completely ratted in the company of friends (which probably means that *you* will rarely touch a drop). Victims drink blithely and unrestrainedly - especially at Regimental Dinner Nights.

OTHER AFFAIRS OF THE HEART AND LOINS

For full membership of the Army Board you should be on your second time around, since a young dolly as a General's wife gives you great street cred and explains why you are constantly falling asleep in Army Board meetings. There are also one or two Army wife 'alternatives' of which you should be aware and which are virtually considered as perks in some appointments (although your *bona fide* wife should be kept strictly *un*aware of these non-taxables).

THE WEEKDAY MINISTRY STAFF OFFICER'S WIFE - Not your real wife, but a well seasoned, glamorous London divorcee with whom you lodge during the week, returning to the ball-and-chain in the Wiltshire cottage (the mortgage is paid for out of your London lodging allowance) at weekends. A smart deal, since you get your leg over throughout the week, you pay the rent in kind, your meals are free, and your wife thinks you are knackered at the weekend because of the punishing hours you work at the Ministry.

DIVORCE - This is a big 'no-no' for the ambitious Army Backstabber, unless you are in a Corps or you are entitled to Star plates on your car (or unless wife No. 2 is outrageously attractive and/or titled, or is a director of a company in which the GOC holds shares).

WIFE-SWAPPING - This is only looked at askance if it becomes public knowledge (members of one Staff College course who indulged in this pastime were given some *fascinating* postings at the end of their year!). At the other end of the scale is the Transport Colonel who took his wife to such a party and came back with a very nice set of socket spanners.

PLANNING YOUR CAREER

As a dedicated Backstabber, you must plan your operation as early as possible. Like greatness, some Backstabbers acquire the art - starting off as Victims until the penny drops half-way through their careers and they have to race to catch up - while with others it is simply inborn. Either way, you should start as early as possible, preferably at Sandhurst. Herewith, your master career plan:

AT SANDHURST - Here you will learn the essential art of bullshit and bluff which will provide the foundation upon which your career will be built. Now is the time to hone your backstabbing skills, using Victims in your platoon to promote your own success. *Do not mention* that you were back-termed, or the real reason why the Arab cadet gave you the Rolex.

LIEUTENANT - Full-blooded young officers will naturally 'Cop heaps of extra duties for bags of high spirits, amid ripping tales of rape and pillage in the Mess'. You should engage in the latter, but let the Victims acquire the former. Make sure you have as many well qualified NCO's as possible and let them run things, while you cultivate business and social contacts for use in retirement. *Do not mention*, at any later date, that your troop only consisted of one Land Rover, one Staff Sergeant, two Sergeants, three Corporals and no responsibility other than tying your bootlaces and appearing for breakfast.

CAPTAIN - Try to gain early promotion to Captain and serve as Aide de Camp (ADC) to a member of the Army Board, a post which holds inherent benefits - viz. meeting all the People Who Matter, and a guaranteed *'Outstanding'* confidential report signed by a 4-Star General (who, with luck, will also have a presentable daughter who will pass muster on the billiard table after the Summer Ball). You must serve as Adjutant of your Regiment and rule with a rod of iron. The men will respect you and it will ensure the approval of the hierarchy. You should end your sojourn as a Captain gloriously, by being selected for Staff College.

AT STAFF COLLEGE - Leave all technical details to the Corps officers who are used to such artisan matters, while you get on with the most important thing - your career. *Do not mention* that you played only individual sports and plagiarised your Commandant's Paper (military thesis) from a 1968 article in *Woman's Own*.

MAJOR - Now is your best opportunity for eliminating the competition for command of the Regiment. Arrange a Royal visit and a humdinger of a Summer Ball. Volunteer your soldiers for everything, and be visibly involved in all aspects of regimental life. Be careful to organise only the events that *really* matter. *Do not mention* that the page 3 birds you arranged for the Subalterns arrived during the Royal visit instead of the Regimental Ball. You will need to complete a Staff job which should be accomplished as the Chief of Staff (COS) to a Brigade. With the current uncertainty in BAOR, you need to pick your post carefully: the UK is convenient for visits to the family and to chums in influential posts in the MOD in London; Hong Kong means a happy wife; Cyprus is no work and all play; and Northern Ireland is a good bet because you need never leave the Ops Room but you will undoubtedly get a gong. *Do not mention* that you were COS to the 53rd Snowdonia Brigade (Welsh Volunteers) at Cwmgwdi Camp, Brecon.

LIEUTENANT COLONEL - For which read everything you did as a Major, but one rank up. As a Staff officer, your Majors will do the work for you, and as Commanding Officer of your Regiment your word is gospel. Impose your personality on all around you (which will not be difficult as there will still be soldiers around who remember your last two tours with the Regiment). The golden rule for Commanding Officers is to remember that there is no such thing as an 'informal' visit from a senior officer. *Do not mention* that your children's boarding school allowance is the only thing keeping you in the Army now that you are pensionable.

COLONEL - As one of the 'fast stream', Backstabber will skip this rank and go straight to . . .

BRIGADIER - You have almost arrived. You will now have a 6-7 bedroom house, a small family saloon staff car with driver, 2 or 3 household staff to do the cleaning, shopping and servicing of the mem-sahib, an entertainments allowance, and occasional use of a helicopter for important engagements. *Do not mention* that you were only in charge of 11th Signal Brigade in Liverpool, or refer to your close personal friendship with a radical northern policeman - either admission would damn you.

GENERAL - The Heinz rank (there are so many varieties). Now is the time to commission your (watercolour) portrait for the Regimental Mess, and to task your ADC to send your potted history to the editor of *Who's Who*. You now have a 9-10 bedroom mansion, a large family saloon staff car with pennant (so that soldiers can salute your driver), and a full complement of household staff so that mem-sahib is free to run the Flower Club. Your entertainments allowance will be almost worthwhile, and you will have a helicopter to ferry you wherever your wife wants to go. At this stage, the political Backstabber will try for an appointment to the Cabinet Office, where judicious flattery at No. 10 (or the advent of a war) will ensure the necessary approval for your appointment to the Army Board.

MEMBERSHIP OF THE ARMY BOARD - Backstabber's goal. Now your (oil) portrait will be commissioned by the Regiment, and you can ask the Regimental Secretary to get your dog, your horse and your wife stuffed and mounted for the regimental museum. You may mention anything you like - any aberrations will be discounted as malicious gossip by your disappointed rivals or the eccentric ramblings of a nice old buffer.

RETIREMENT - Now is the time to accept a City directorship, take a rod on the Spey, and become Colonel Commandant of the Regiment. You may also be offered this appointment by a couple of the Corps: do not pooh-pooh them, even if they come from the Pioneer or Catering Corps (for you will want a marquee and a buffet when your daughter gets married). No subject is unmentionable - and the Sun pays well for 'informed' opinions.

COURSE BLADEMANSHIP

Backstabber's master plan includes several important career courses that must be attended - Staff College being the pre-eminent example. Thereafter most officers spend the majority of their time on courses rather than on regimental duties. This is good Army strategy, for it means that the real business of soldiering is administered by efficient Warrant Officers and Sergeants, leaving proper careers to be forged in the halls of military academies.

THE BACKSTABBER'S TEN-POINT GUIDE TO COURSE BLADESMANSHIP

BACKSTABBER	GOOD STUDENT	VICTIM	BAD STUDENT	COURSE JOKE
Point One - Motivation				
Locks classroom to ensure being in first next day	Arrives in class before tutor	Has an excuse for his lateness	Sleeps in class	Is absent (no-one told him where to go)
Point Two - Interest in Course				
Asks relevant questions but ignores answers	Nods occasionally as if he has read the precis	Fixes tutor with hypnotic stare	Stares blankly into space	Fixes clock with hypnotic stare
Point Three - Sense of Proportion and Humour				
Quotes Evelyn Waugh & Wilde	Quotes the Goons	Laughs at tutor's jokes	Laughs at anything	Is subject of tutor's jokes
Point Four - Personal Appearance				
Wears correct dress at all times	Wears uniform with matching tie and handkerchief	Has own dress	Wears wife's dress	Wears nappy underneath
Point Five - Intellectual Curiosity				
Wants to know how technical concepts affect his career	Wants to know what a technical concept is	Wants to know what concept means	Wants to know where he is and what day it is	What ??
Point Six - Intellectual Ability				
Uses terms like *vis a vis & per se*	Writes, using joined up letters	Prints using wax crayons	Eats wax crayons	Floats in water
Point Seven - Participation in Discussions				
Ignores syndicate, speaks only to tutor	Participates fully in all periods	Is ignored by syndicate & tutor	Invents red herrings	Eats red herrings

Point Eight - Literacy				
Will discourse on Solzhenitsyn	Quotes Liddell-Hart	Secretly enjoys Enid Blyton	Memorises road signs	Believes the *Sun*
Point Nine - Technical Ability				
Can convert parking meters to accept ECU's	Is *au fait* with both imperial and metric units	Thinks 'mils' are for grinding coffee	Confused by numbers	Often wires himself up to the mains
Point Ten - Degree of Service Orientation				
Knows difference between Aid to the Civil Power and a coup	Accepts his regimental history as gospel	Believes that his boss 'always gets it right'	Thinks he has a future in the Army	Believes the cavalry know what they are talking about

AND FINALLY . . .

Even in such an amoral art as backstabbing, there are certain rules which must be observed in order to survive the game to the bitter end. The golden rule is: Backstabbing is a covert art - *never* get caught (if you do, try and point the finger elsewhere - preferably back at your accuser). Keep your bayonet dry and trust no-one but the reflection in your mirror. Lastly, remember that a back turned is a back stabbed, and a pat on the back is merely a recce for a blade!

May the spirit of St Brutus ensure that you get your just rewards.